# The Neglected Trinity

# The Neglected Trinity

Recovering from Theological Amnesia

*Steven Tsoukalas*

CASCADE *Books* · Eugene, Oregon

THE NEGLECTED TRINITY
Recovering from Theological Amnesia

Cascade Books
An Imprint of Wipf and Stock Publishers
199 W. 8th Ave., Suite 3
Eugene, OR 97401

www.wipfandstock.com

PAPERBACK ISBN: 978-1-7252-9472-1
HARDCOVER ISBN: 978-1-7252-9473-8
EBOOK ISBN: 978-1-7252-9474-5

*Cataloguing-in-Publication data:*

Names: Tsoukalas, Steven, 1956–.

Title: The neglected Trinity : recovering from theological amnesia / Steven Tsoukalas.

Description: Eugene, OR: Cascade Books, 2021 | Includes bibliographical references and index.

Identifiers: ISBN 978-1-7252-9472-1 (paperback) | ISBN 978-1-7252-9473-8 (hardcover) | ISBN 978-1-7252-9474-5 (ebook)

Subjects: LCSH: Trinity | Trinity—Criticism, interpretation, etc. | Trinity—History of doctrines | God (Christianity)

Classification: BT111.3 T76 2021 (print) | BT111.3 (ebook)

*For Noël and Elise*

*"God is the Trinity, and the Trinity is God"*
—THOMAS F. TORRANCE

# Table of Contents

# Preface

An abundant and holy life uncompromisingly entails a deep knowledge of and relationship with the triune God through the Lord of Glory, Jesus Christ. It must not be any other way. It must be trinitarian.

The reason I have written this brief book on the doctrine of the Trinity is because many of us in the church have forgotten it, or because we think of it as something to put on the shelf and hardly, if ever, refer to it or think about it.

Change is drastically needed.

I am not being melodramatic when I say that the situation is drastic. The insidious thing about it is that this amnesia lies in a menacing way *underneath the surface*. We do not even know how sick we are when it comes to the God who reveals himself to us and for us as triune and *only* as triune.

By the grace of the Holy Trinity, we through the enabling of God the Holy Spirit can *really* know the Lord Jesus, and therefore at the very same time know the Father. He who in the power of his Holy Spirit came for us did not come to us empty and with nothing to reveal. The Lord Jesus comes in the riches of his own glory that he shares with the Father so that we might have life, and have it abundantly.

The chapters of this book, with the exception of the introduction and the last chapter, contain a "Basics" section and a "Beyond the Basics" section, each with a few discussion topics for thoughtful meditation. Feel free to read only the "Basics" sections or to read both sections!

In the introduction I bring attention to very important issues. Some of the issues are not so positive. They may surprise you, as they did me when I first heard of them. They reveal certain ills in the way many of us view "God" (the quote marks are intentional!) and the way many of us worship. Other issues are positive but may be unknown to many of us. Once known, they deepen our knowledge of and relationship with the Holy Trinity, and therefore enrich our worship.

Chapter 1 focuses first on a basic understanding of the doctrine of the Trinity. So the "Basics" is a "just the facts, please" section, outlining the scriptural reasons for the doctrine. I have often used this section for Sunday school classes, college and seminary classes, one-on-one discipleship, and in the many years of visiting the meeting places of several pseudo-Christian religions in order to evangelize their adherents. With "Beyond the Basics" we go deeper, outlining several doctrinal notions that indeed bring us "beyond."

In the next three chapters we witness the unfolding of the revelation of the triune God as we study who the three divine persons are, and better understand why it is that the three persons are the one Holy Trinity.

Chapter 2 looks into who God the Father—the first person of the Trinity—is. God the Father is often overlooked in formal study, so we do well to know him better in order to be blessed with a deeper relationship with him.

Chapter 3 focuses on the second person of the triune God, the Lord Jesus Christ. Here we are concerned with his deity and humanity, exploring what he has done for us and for our salvation.

Chapter 4 engages the person of the Holy Spirit, the third person of the Trinity, the one who revealed himself in power and with signs and wonders as the Christian church came into being. The Holy Spirit, along with the Father and the Son, is both a person and true deity.

Chapter 5 brings it all together. There we examine several Christian doctrines and some important issues in Christian theology, which includes worship, placing them where they rightly belong—in the life of the Holy Trinity. Since Christian theology must be *trinitarian* theology, the church's worship should be trinitarian.

There is a glossary of terms found at the end of the book. It provides definitions and explanations of terms.

Readers can also consult the Nicene Creed and the Creed of Chalcedon, found in the appendix. These are two very important creeds for the Christian church throughout the whole world and for all times—past, present, and future.

Let's begin!

# Introduction

## What Happened to the Doctrine of the Trinity?

Years ago I invited two Jehovah's Witnesses elders to my home for doctrinal conversation. (As you may know, the Jehovah's Witnesses vehemently deny the doctrine of the Trinity.) After a bit of get-to-know-you conversation, the deep discussion began. They said that the Trinity doctrine is not only unreasonable but is a pagan doctrine. At that point I asked them if they would like to hear an explanation of the doctrine of the Trinity. They said yes. After I finished with an explanation, one of the elders exclaimed, "I have been at this for forty years, and I have *never* heard an explanation like *that*! I have heard explanations like, 'They are the same person'; 'The three are one'; 'There are three Gods, yet one God'; 'All three are the same'; 'There is one person who becomes another person who becomes another person.'" I then stated, "Well shame on us!" Imagine? Forty years and he has never heard a right explanation of the doctrine of the Trinity!

What happened to the doctrine of the Trinity that was so strongly emphasized in the early church? Since the Holy Trinity—the Father and the Son and the Holy Spirit—is the one and only God, why is the Trinity and the doctrine of the Trinity largely missing in the life and faith of the church?

Theologian Thomas F. Torrance put it this way:

> In modern times it is unfortunately the case that the enormous importance of the doctrine of the Trinity, and its revolutionary implications, have tended to be

1

lost from sight, and sometimes to be treated as rather irrelevant, or only of peripheral significance for Christian
faith and living. Much of the reason for this is that people
have worked for so long in the Western World with a notion of God who is somehow inertially detached[1] from
this world, exalted inaccessibly above it, and remote
from our creaturely cries and prayers. And so in Western[2] theology particularly it has become too common for
theologians to separate the doctrine of the one God from
the doctrine of the triune God.[3]

That certainly is a mouthful! Let's explore the above quotation.

## The Doctrine Is Important

First, the doctrine of the Trinity and the one to whom it points (the
triune God) is of "enormous importance." Why? It is of enormous
necessity that we worship the Holy Trinity.

Second, the doctrine of the Trinity has revolutionary implications for the life of the church. Do we really grasp that the three
distinct persons of the Trinity—Father, Son, and Holy Spirit—from
the very beginning of the Bible offer themselves to us and for us
in a way that we may know them as they have revealed themselves
to us as the one God? In that very revelation of the triune God to
us, in Christ and in the Scriptures, we are called to worship him
according to that revelation, to live according to that revelation.

Third, the Holy Trinity comes to humanity in mission. The
triune God offers himself for the salvation of all who call upon
him. Since humanity relationally has fallen away from him, God
reveals himself in the context of rescuing humanity from its state
of alienation from him. In short, the triune God is *the* missionary
who comes to save the lost. The church must not lose sight of this.

---

1. Referring to the view that God is detached from the world and inactive
in it.

2. See the Glossary, "Western and Eastern Traditions."

3. Torrance, *Christian Doctrine*, 8–9. As regards this last sentence from Torrance, see the section in this introduction entitled "Theology Hates Partitions."

# Lost from Sight

The doctrine of the Trinity has indeed been "lost from sight" and "treated as rather irrelevant." Sadly, the doctrine on a large scale has been relegated to "peripheral significance." One reason (though there are several) is that many of us do not take the time to be in conversation with the great minds of the early church (for example, in the second through fifth centuries). Though there are certain traditions of the Christian church that have a robust acknowledgement of the Holy Trinity, they are in my experience more the exception than the norm. In my many years as a Christian, I have never heard a sermon on the doctrine of the Trinity. Moreover, I hardly ever hear the words "Trinity" or "triune God." And what about recitation and study of the Nicene Creed? We have ignored[4] or have relegated to the periphery this magnificent confession of the early church that provides for us an articulation of the substance of the faith found in the Bible.

But there is another way in which the doctrine of the Trinity becomes lost, irrelevant, or relegated to the periphery for Christian faith and living. In our worship times there may be mention of the Trinity or of the Father and the Son and the Holy Spirit, but commonly it is of passing significance. Perhaps you might see that as a positive step in the right direction. It can be if it is the first step, but unfortunately it often stops there. One mention is not enough. Worshipful acknowledgement of the Trinity must flood our worship. How is this done? I come now to the issue of theological predicates.

---

4. Roman Catholic theologian Karl Rahner, lamenting the lack of trinitarian doctrine, stated, "[S]hould the doctrine of the Trinity have to be dropped as false, the major part of religious literature could well remain virtually unchanged" (*The Trinity*, 10–11).

## Theological Predicates

Throughout worship there should be an acknowledgement of the Trinity that emphasizes both the oneness and the distinctness of the three persons. This is done by employing predicates.

Don't let the word scare you. Theological predicates are words used to describe a subject, for our purpose "God."

To get used to the idea of predicates, consider three phrases. I will place the predicates in italics so you can quickly identify them: the *red* car; Jane *the professor*; Bill *the carpenter*. The words car, Jane, and Bill by themselves can be void of personal meaning without predicates. I might say to someone, "Bill came over." "Bill *who?*" comes the reply of my conversation partner. Predicates are significant because they define the subject and give specific answers to the questions, What car? What Jane? What Bill?

Though we do not *always* need to use predicates for "God," it is good to do if we suspect that confusion will result on the parts of our listeners. Now let's bring proper predicates to the word "God": *triune* God; God *the Father*; God *the Son*; God *the Holy Spirit*. These are vitally important to employ because in many contexts, listeners not nuanced in theology could end up with the idea of an abstract (and therefore ultimately meaningless) conception of God. The word "God" can be an empty slogan, and oftentimes when people employ the word, it is.[5]

Countless times there occurs in Christian articulation and prayer a careless use of the word "God." What "God" are we talking about? Moreover, what of prayers like this: "O God . . . thank you for your incarnation." Exactly which person of the Holy Trinity are we talking about? Might a person think that the Father incarnated? Or this: "Heavenly Father . . . thank you that you died on the cross." These kinds of prayers are uttered by well-meaning followers of Christ, but nonetheless they are at least problematic. They fail to distinguish properly the three persons of the Trinity and even

---

5. One need only watch television news and after-game interviews to witness this.

confuse their roles. "So what?" you might be thinking. "What does it matter?"

The Holy Trinity matters! People can be, and are, led astray by theological speech that is not accurate and precise. This takes us to our next section.

## "GAWP"

In the Bible and in the early church we find a certain posture, the description of which I have borrowed from Torrance: "Godliness with Accuracy; Worship with Precision." The way I remember this phrase is to take the word "GAWK" (to stare) and replace the K with a P; thus, GAWP: Godliness with Accuracy; Worship with Precision.[6] Allow me to state obvious reasons for the need to strive for GAWP.

Take the phrase "God and Jesus." Though biblical, it still takes some theologizing to understand it. Yet, do we ever take the time to understand the phrase biblically-theologically?[7] What about Christians new to the faith (or even older ones) who are not far along in accurate and therefore godly and worshipful doctrinal understanding? What might this phrase, left theologically un-touched, communicate to those among us who are not Christians? It could communicate this: "Well, there is God; and there is also Jesus." They will make the erroneous conclusion that Jesus is not God the Son.

To illustrate, I recall years ago a person in a gathering chal-lenging a pastor with this: "When we pray, we pray to God. We don't pray to Jesus. We pray to God. Jesus is not God; he's the Son of God." If this person had been discipled with emphasis on proper predicates for the words she was using, "God the Father" and "God

6. GAWP should therefore be the posture in which we select worship songs, give testimonies, evangelize, preach, teach, converse, and pray.

7. As an exercise, turn to one of Paul's writings in the New Testament. Look somewhere in the middle of the book or letter and locate "God." You will see many instances where "God" has no predicate. But note that Paul has already given us the predicate for "God" in the first few verses of the book or letter!

the Son" would have permeated her understanding and would have prevented her from uttering serious heresy.[8] Predicates are uncompromisingly important. They are important because they point to the ultimate personal reality of the triune God, and we must strive to employ them.

To use predicates in worship and in all kinds of Christian "speak" is good for us, good for others, and good for the church worldwide. It fosters godliness with accuracy and worship with precision and therefore, most important of all, honors the triune God who reveals himself specially as Father, Son, and Holy Spirit; and because he has done so, it is incumbent upon us by the enabling grace of God the Holy Spirit to "get it right" in order to honor properly the Holy Trinity.

## Trinity as Theological Paradigm

There is yet another life-giving doctrine or model involving the Holy Trinity: All doctrine, all living, all our Christian articulations and prayers, *take place within the life of the Trinity*. This is the trinitarian paradigm that should be the means of control for all our theology.

Here are some examples (more follow as this book unfolds) of the doctrine of the Trinity as the controlling paradigm for theology.

First, what about all my above-mentioned "we must"s and "we should"s? Are these left to our own power? No. It is only by the enabling grace and indwelling presence of God the Holy Spirit that we fulfill the "must" and the "should." Left to ourselves we can do nothing that truly pleases God the Father. But how often have we heard and how often have we said the "dos" and the "don'ts" without clear, precise teaching that it is God the Holy Spirit who, with the Father and the Son, provides the enabling to do and don't? If the doctrine of the Trinity were the controlling center for all

---

8. Soon after, I had a good conversation with this person. She acknowledged who Jesus truly is.

doctrine, we would not slide into this "pull yourself up by your own power" mentality.

Second, let us take the doctrine of the virgin conception and birth of the Lord Jesus Christ. By the grace of the Holy Spirit, the doctrine must not be seen as a doctrine isolated from other doctrines, and must not be isolated from its very foundation and divine context, the triune God. Notice the Trinity here: God the Father sends God the Son (the "Word" mentioned in John 1:1) to incarnate among us (John 1:14; 3:16) in the womb of the virgin Mary by the agency of God the Holy Spirit (Matt 1:18, 20). If we read the Bible in this trinitarian way, we will be well on our way to biblical understanding that honors the Holy Trinity.

## Theology Hates Partitions

This section goes hand in hand with the previous section. If theology must be understood in the trinitarian paradigm (within the life of the Trinity), then theology hates partitioning; that is, theology is not done well if it severs or isolates doctrines from each other and severs doctrines from the Holy Trinity.

Athanasius, following the teaching of the apostles, models for Christians the way to do theology. Athanasius modeled for us the truth that theology hates partitioning. All doctrine and theological events themselves should not be isolated doctrines and events, that is, torn apart from the very foundation upon which they stand—the Trinity. Trinitarian-based theology *by definition* does not separate or sever doctrines from the life of the triune God.

One quite unfortunate, and fatal, example of partition in theology is the deep-rooted tendency first to talk of "God" and only after that to talk of Trinity? By doing so, are we communicating to others who are not deeply rooted in Christian theology that "God" can be thought of apart from Trinity? Moreover, by not using proper predicates for "God," could we be aiding the confusion of others who might already have an abstract and generic view of "God" void of any specific personal meaning? This kind of theology can also lead to seeing the "one God" essentially as a separate category from the Holy Trinity,[9] rather than seeing the one God as[10] the Holy Trinity and the Holy Trinity as the one God. As Torrance puts it, "God is the Trinity, and the Trinity is God."[11] In our minds and expressions of worship, there should not be any concept of "God" first, and then only after that, Trinity.

On the positive side, non-partitive trinitarian-based theology cannot have the Father without the Son, nor the Son without the Father, nor the Holy Spirit without the Son and the Father, nor the Father and the Son without the Holy Spirit. Each person is precisely what each person is in eternal relation to the other persons.

9. A tragic symptom of this partitioning occurs when people answer yes to the question, "Do Christians and Muslims worship the same God?" (What follows also applies to the question of whether Christians and [non-Messianic] Jews worship the same God.) Here, proponents of "the same God" separate the doctrine of "the one God" from the Trinity, at best relegating the doctrine of the Trinity to secondary importance. They also fail to apply proper predicates to "God." Since the triune God is the only God that truly is, the way rightly to phrase the question is this: "Do Christians and Muslims worship the triune God?" In other words, phrasing the question in the popular, common way is erroneous from the start. What "God" are we talking about? Muslims holding to the Qur'an deny the Trinity and therefore deny the true and living triune God. Further, "same God" proponents often isolate the doctrine of Jesus from their notions of "God," thereby making Jesus ultimately unimportant to the identity of "God." This is due largely to the "great gulf," which I explain in the next section. Additionally, perhaps this question cuts better at the heart of the issue: "Do Christians and Muslims and Jews worship God the Father?" As we shall see later on, no one can truly and rightly worship the Father apart from Jesus and in communion with God the Holy Spirit. For an expanded explanation of these and other issues, see Tsoukalas, "Do Christians and Muslims."

10. Should we confess three persons in one God or three persons as one God? One God in three persons or one God as three persons? These two prepositions say a lot about how a person thinks of the Trinity. Though we should not sever fellowship over this question, it still remains worthy of consideration because we are talking about the triune God! I favor "as" because "three persons in one God" communicates that the three persons are in another something, and "one God in three persons" communicates another something that is in the three persons. "As" vividly and dynamically emphasizes the relations of all the three persons in the contexts of the doctrines of homo-ousios and peri-choresis.

11. Torrance, Trinitarian Faith, 330.

Therefore, the distinct doctrines of each of the persons of the Trinity must be expressed in fully trinitarian fashion.

By the enabling grace of God the Holy Spirit, we must understand each of the distinct persons as they have been revealed to us. Though it is necessary to study and to learn about the Father in distinction from the Son and the Holy Spirit, the Father must always be understood as Father *in union with* the Son and the Spirit. Failure to express theology in this non-partitive trinitarian way is a major problem in the Christian church today. And there are symptoms stemming from this, often going undetected by the majority of Christians because our ongoing practice, whether consciously or unconsciously, is to isolate the Son from the Father and the Spirit. But as we shall see later on, the doctrine of *homo-ousios* forbids that practice.

What follows is the root of several problems in theology (which includes worship) today—the "great gulf."

## The "Great Gulf"

The second half of Torrance's words speaks about (1) the error of seeing "God" detached from this world, inaccessible, and remote from us; and (2) the tendency in Western theology to "separate the doctrine of the one God from the doctrine of the triune God."[12]

Let's look at the first point, but I first must mention something so there won't be confusion over the issue. There of course is in Scripture the confession of the transcendence of the LORD: The LORD is holy, holy, holy (Isa 6:3), the high and exalted One who dwells in a high and holy place (Isa 57:15; 33:5), and heaven is his

---

12. Many modern books on theology have a chapter on "God" and/or "The Attributes of God" and *then* a chapter on "The Trinity." See Charles Hodge, *Systematic Theology* (vol. 1); A. A. Hodge, *Outlines*; Erickson, *Christian Theology*; Bavinck, *Doctrine of God*; and Wiley and Culbertson, *Introduction*. See also Thomas Aquinas, who lived in the thirteenth century. In his *Summa*, he first has a section on the one God (I.2–26), followed by a section on the Trinity (I.27–43). Perhaps this led Aquinas to state, "Even if the personal properties of the three Persons are abstracted by our mind, nevertheless there will remain in our thoughts the one Personality of God, as the Jews consider" (III.3.3. ad. 2).

throne and the earth his footstool (Isa 66:1). He revealed himself to Moses as "I AM" (Exod 3:14). For these reasons the LORD transcends us as infinite personal being and worthy to be praised. The Scriptures tirelessly describe the LORD's transcendence. So yes, the LORD is transcendent, high and exalted.

However, oftentimes we worship as if that is all there is to it. The mindset in the way we pray evidences this habitual frame of mind lurking under the surface: "God is up there; we are down here." This theological illness underlies what we think and therefore how we worship, how we pray, and what we say about "God." There is in our thinking an abstract, non-concrete, non-trinitarian "God" (void of predicates) who is utterly displaced from us across an unbridgeable great gulf.

This simple chart illustrates:

"God"

*A Great Gulf Exists between "God"
and Humanity*

Us

On the second point, a result of great gulfism is the notion of "God." And then only *after* that, Trinity.[13] Here the doctrine of the Trinity is either a human-concocted doctrine insufficiently pointing to the one utterly transcendent "God," or a doctrine of secondary importance.[14] Great gulfism plagues us by lying quietly (sometimes not so quietly) underneath the surface so as to be presumed *unconsciously* in our thinking, theologizing, praying, preaching, and living. Put simply, God is far away; beyond reach.

13. As mentioned in the previous note, theology books often proceed, evidenced by chapter divisions, with this erroneous model.

14. Great gulfism also is the foundation for the conclusion that Christians and Muslims worship the same "God" (see the note addressing this in the previous section ["Theology Hates Partitions"]). This happens when people first begin with either an abstract notion of "God" or a non-triune notion of "God" and then proceed to answer "yes" in conclusion. This way of thinking replaces the truth that God is the Trinity and the Trinity is God.

To emphasize what was said before, there is no "God" and *then* the Trinity—God *is* the Holy Trinity, and the Holy Trinity *is* God, revealed to us in the concrete material reality of Jesus in space and time—in history. Through him and by his Holy Spirit we know the triune God as intimately near to us and in us through God the Holy Spirit. The Holy Trinity is *really* present with us, and *for* us.

The notion of great gulfism arguably is the most damaging of thoughts within the Christian camp. I shall have more to say on this later, but for now let us consider the obvious in answer to this way of thinking. Was not the LORD *with* his people the ancient Israelites? Throughout the Old Testament there is a resounding "Yes!" Here are a few examples of many. The LORD appeared to Moses (Exod 3) and to Joshua (Josh 5). The LORD states that he is *with* his covenant people (Isa 43:2, 5). In Exodus 40:34–38 we read that the LORD's glory filled the tabernacle. With the coming of the Lord Jesus the presence of the LORD was pushed to the most profound and concrete sense, for as John states, "The Word [the pre-incarnate God the Son, the Logos of John 1:1] became flesh, and dwelt [tabernacled!] among us" (John 1:14), indicating that with Jesus we *really*, in time and space, have Immanuel, God *with* us (Matt 1:23). This blessed truth applies to us today, because Jesus as God the Son says he will be *with* us always (Matt 28:20).

## Worship, Salvation, and Evangelism Grounded in the Life of the Triune God

The Holy Trinity is both the ground and source of life and worship for the church. The church is built upon the foundation of the apostles (apostolic tradition), with Jesus himself as the cornerstone (Eph 2:20).

Several early church theologians, and I think especially of Athanasius (fourth century), took time to express doctrine in the context of the triune God and Jesus's relation to the Father; and this in the context of worshipful adoration, salvation, and the spread of the gospel. This sets the stage for one of the most important words expressed in the early church, to which we now turn.

## Homo-ousios

Note this word and its significance, for it provides for us the substance/foundation of Christianity! Precise worship, a precise view of salvation, and rightly construed evangelism depend upon the biblical fact that the Son is *homoousion to patri*: "one being[15] with the Father." In the Nicene Creed (and the Nicene-Constantino-politan Creed) the Greek word *homo-ousios* communicates the biblical-theological truth that Jesus is "God from God . . . true God from true God." To put it succinctly, Jesus shares the same being (nature) with the Father.[16] In worshipful language the framers of the creed expressed the equality of the Son with the Father, for the Son became incarnate, says the creed, "for us and for our salvation."

Much was at stake for anyone who denied the equality (*homo-ousios*) of Jesus with the Father. Worship, salvation, and evangelism would not be what the apostolic tradition taught if *homo-ousios* was rejected; and one popular heretic would do just that!

Athanasius and the early church fought against a heretic (false teacher) named Arius of Alexandria (fourth century) who, like today's Jehovah's Witnesses, denied that Jesus is God the Son. Jesus in his pre-existence, said Arius, was *not* of the same nature as the Father, but rather was *hetero-ousios* (a different nature) compared to the Father, and was the first creature created by the Father. In setting forth this view Arius referred to "the Word" (Greek *logos*) in John 1:1 as a *created* being. Instead of seeing the Logos as the eternal and pre-existent God the Son and the incarnate Jesus as God the Son become man, Arius denied Jesus's true deity.

---

15. Or, as some modern translations of the creed read, "con-substantial with the Father."

16. In Chapter 3, I examine John 1:1, the third phrase of which reads "and the Word was God." This explicitly teaches that the Logos of the Father shares with the Father the nature of deity.

Athanasius in his brief but amazing treatise entitled *On Luke 10:22*[17] argued strongly and uncompromisingly for the full deity of Jesus. I encourage you to read this brief work. In it you will find many verses from the Gospel of John. This is because the Gospel of John thoroughly portrays Jesus as the Son of God the Father, and God the Son (more on this in Chapter 3). Athanasius in his various works had Arianism in mind and passionately refuted it. He was actively involved in the Council of Nicaea (AD 325) and its pronouncement against Arius and others who denied the full deity of Jesus.

About forty-six years later (AD 381), early church theologians at the Council of Constantinople added to the end of the Nicene Creed a section on the Holy Spirit, confessing him as "the Lord, the giver of life. . . . With the Father and the Son he is worshiped and glorified." The Nicene-Constantinopolitan Creed of AD 381 was not developed out of thin air. Rather, the theologians who composed it were faithful to the orthodoxy *already revealed* (this is important!) in the Scriptures. Moreover, they were concerned to develop the creed in the context of worship, salvation, and the proclamation of the gospel.

How is it that worship, salvation, and the proclamation of the gospel depend upon Jesus being equal in nature (*homo-ousios*) with the Father? To set the stage for the answer to this question is a way of thinking that early church theologians, with Athanasius as primary among them,[18] adopted (so should we!): If A, then what about B?[19] To place this in our context, if Jesus is not God

17. Where Jesus said, "No one knows who the Son is except the Father, and who the Father is except the Son, and anyone to whom the Son wills to reveal *him* [the Father]." Athanasius in this work stressed continuously that the Son is "proper" to the Father. By "proper" Athanasius meant that Jesus, God the Logos incarnate, is all that the Father is, except Father.

18. This is not to say that theologians before the time of Athanasius (fourth century) had no clue of the importance of the equality of the Father and the Son (and the Holy Spirit). Irenaeus (second century) argued against heretics that *only God can reveal God*, and that therefore Jesus as God the Son properly and alone (with the Holy Spirit) reveals God the Father.

19. Taken from Thomas F. Torrance.

the Son who shares in the very nature of the Father, then what about worship, salvation, and evangelism? Put in more detail, if Jesus is not God by nature (and also fully man; more on this in a later chapter), how can the triune God *himself* save us? Further, if Jesus is not fully God by nature but just a fantastic messenger of God the Father, how can we, in personally concrete fashion with God the Son himself, worship the Father? Indeed, how is it that we can *really* know the Father personally as he comes to us in Jesus? Additionally, can we *really* communicate the concretely personal divine reality of the gospel without Jesus as God the Son coming to reveal the Father to us in history?

## In Closing

The triunely personal God—the Father and the Son and the Holy Spirit—is the *only* God that truly is. That being the case, the Holy Trinity should not be given just a passing nod of the head at the end of a sermon or worship (if it is mentioned at all). Rather, worshipful adoration of the Holy Trinity should permeate our worship. By the grace of the Holy Spirit, let us labor to learn the doctrine of the Trinity and absorb the living and dynamic reality of the Father and the Son and the Holy Spirit.

## Discussion

1. Has the notion of the "great gulf" affected you? Give an example or two.

2. Look at Ephesians 2:18–22 and see Paul's placing of doctrine directly in the life of the Trinity. Expound upon his teaching—how the three distinct persons of the Trinity act in the building of the church. Note: the predicate for "God" in this passage has already been given to us by Paul. See Ephesians 1:2.

CHAPTER 1

# The Doctrine of the Trinity

What follows first is a concise explanation of the doctrine of the Trinity. In the "Beyond the Basics" section we explore the doctrine of the Trinity more deeply, in part pointing to the living reality of the triune God in the context of salvation (who he is *for* us), proclamation, and worship.

## The Basics

Let's first understand *what* the doctrine of the Trinity is—to apprehend it, to grasp it scripturally in a "bare bones" way.

### Grasping Scripturally the Doctrine of the Trinity

First on the list is to get some presuppositions on the table. Presuppositions are not necessarily a bad thing. Many, including the three below, can be defended successfully. However, because of the specific subject of this book, we will not venture into a detailed defense.

A presupposition is something assumed or taken for granted. Before discussing the doctrine of the Trinity we need to state three presuppositions:

1. The Bible is the Word of the triune God.

2. The triune God is eternal in being; perfect, flawless, without contradiction, etc.

3. Humanity is finite; created, imperfect, and flawed.

Therefore, we cannot *completely comprehend how* the one God is the Father and the Son and the Holy Spirit (because of #2 and #3). We can, however, *truly apprehend that* the one God is the Father and the Son and the Holy Spirit (because of #1).

Here is the doctrine in three sentences:

1. There is one God (Isa 43:10).

2. The Father is called God (2 Pet 1:17); the Son is called God (John 20:28); and the Holy Spirit is called God (1 Cor 3:16; 6:19).

3. The three distinct persons are the one triune God (Matt 28:19).

## Explanation

Notice the use of the phrases *completely comprehend how* and *truly apprehend that*. To completely comprehend something means to understand it *fully*, that is, to know *everything* about it. For example, is anyone able to comprehend fully the "how" of a rose as it exists in a field in relation to all other things around it? Even though we cannot, we nonetheless can truly apprehend (grasp, take hold of mentally) that an object called a rose exists in a field in relation to all other things around it, and therefore can comprehend it in limited fashion. In the same fashion, we as finite creatures (#3) will never completely comprehend how the Holy Trinity "is" because the triune God is eternal, perfect, and inexhaustible as personal being (#2); but we can truly apprehend what the Bible teaches (#1) and therefore in some measure know *that* God is Trinity, and *in some measure* comprehend.

The first sentence of the doctrine reads, "There is one God." In Isaiah 43:10 we read, "You are my witnesses . . . that you may know and believe me and understand that I am he. Before me there was no God formed; and there will be none after me." So there is one God—only one God by nature (cf. Gal 4:8). Christians are monotheists. Monotheism is the belief that only one God truly is.

Now for the second sentence.

In the New Testament we have three persons, and each is called God.

The Father is called God. Second Peter 1:17 refers to "God the Father."

The Son (Jesus) is called God. In John 20:28, Thomas makes one of the greatest confessions about Jesus, which also should be on our lips. Thomas said to Jesus, "My Lord and my God."

The Holy Spirit is called God. Keep in mind this very important theme in the Old Testament: the divine presence. The LORD was "with" his people. See Isaiah 43:2, 5: "When you pass through the waters, I will be with you"; "Do not fear, for I am with you." The theme of divine presence is expressed with the cloud filling the tabernacle or dwelling place, and that the glory of the LORD filled the dwelling place (Exod 40:34–38). Amazingly, Paul applies the theme of divine presence to the Holy Spirit. In 1 Corinthians 6:19 he states, "Don't you all know that your body is a temple of the Holy Spirit who is in you?" (my translation). Paul is referring to the body of believers, which is called the body of Christ (1 Cor 12:27). To put it succinctly, God the Holy Spirit is himself the personal divine presence in the temple that is the body of Christ (cf. 1 Cor 3:16), the church.[1]

Our third sentence is a bit involved, but not out of reach! Let's look at Matthew 28:19 together. The last portion of the verse reads "the name of the Father and the Son and the Holy Spirit." Now let's look at a rule of Greek grammar: When two or more singular personal nouns (not proper names) are separated by "and" and are preceded by the definite article "the," we have two or more distinct nouns.[2] Thankfully we can see this rule applied using an English

---

1. See also 2 Corinthians 3:18: "But we all, with unveiled faces, looking as in a mirror at the glory of the Lord, are being transformed into the same image from glory to glory, just as from the Lord, the Spirit." Here Paul calls the Holy Spirit "the Lord" of the Exodus story.

2. You can see this rule and five other rules in Sharp, *Remarks*.

translation. In the phrase "of the Father and the Son and the Holy Spirit," do we have two or more nouns? Yes: Father, Son, and Holy Spirit. Are they each separated by "and"? Yes. Do each of the nouns have the definite article "the" before them? Yes. This means that we have three distinct nouns, in this case persons. So the three distinct persons *are* the one[3] triune God, the one divine "name."

## Discussion

1. Explain the doctrine of the Trinity with the Scripture verses. Use predicates!

2. This one is challenging. Spend some time thinking through the doctrine of the Trinity and utilize trinitarian theology (the trinitarian paradigm) to interpret John 14:6. After you do this, take some other biblical verses or passages and expound upon them in the same way.

### Beyond the Basics

Here we look more deeply into Matthew 28:19. We will also discover the richness of two theological terms that bring into light the magnificent revelation of the Holy Trinity to us and for us.

### AIRO

With the phrase "the name of the Father and the Son and the Holy Spirit," how should we understand "name"? First, note that the three distinct persons *are*[4] the *one* "name." Second, "name" in Matthew 28:19 does not refer to a name of a person (like the names Paul, Peter, Alice). Third, I use the acronym AIRO to help identify four meanings for "name" in the verse (which overlap): Authority;

---

3. By virtue of both *homo-ousios* and *peri-choresis*. See the "Beyond the Basics" section for more explanation.

4. "Are" denoting "is-ness" (see the Glossary, "Being").

Identity; Reputation; Ownership. Though there are several biblical examples substantiating AIRO, here are a few for each.

## Authority

To be "called by the name of the LORD" evidences his authority over those he has called. Second Chronicles 7:14: "[If] my people, who are called by my name humble themselves." The state of humbleness before the LORD is a state of mind and heart stemming from a confession of his authority. Isaiah 30:30 reads, "The LORD will cause his voice of authority to be heard." And in Jeremiah 14:14–15 false prophets were prophesying lies "in my name." They do this, says the LORD, even though "I have neither sent them nor commanded them" (v. 14), implying authority.

## Identity

In the Bible "name" also identifies who someone is, that is, identifies the characteristics or attributes of someone. We see this with Nabal ("fool") in 1 Samuel 25:25 and with Jacob ("he who seizes the heel"; "he who replaces/supplants") in Genesis 25:26. Jacob then acts true to his name, which reveals a particular characteristic: "Is he not rightly named Jacob, for he has supplanted me these two times" (Gen 27:36). In the New Testament, the name John means "favored of the LORD." The name Jesus means "YHWH is savior." Matthew 1:21 reads, "You shall call his name Jesus, for he will save his people from their sins." Based upon the above examples we also see that someone *is* as someone *does*; and someone *does* as someone *is*.

## Reputation

See Daniel 9:19 ("Your [God's] city and your people are called by your name") and look at the surrounding verses, which communicate the reputation, the mighty acts, of the LORD. Herod "heard" of what Jesus was doing because "His name had become well known"

(Mark 6:14). "Blessed are you when men . . . scorn your name as evil" (Luke 6:22). Jesus chose Saul (later Paul) to "bear my name[5] before the Gentiles and kings and the sons of Israel" (Acts 9:15). Saul then preaches that Jesus is the Son of God (v. 20); he proclaims Jesus's reputation.

### Ownership

In 2 Chronicles 7:14 the LORD speaks of "my people who are called by my name." Here ownership and name are equated. In Isaiah 43:21 the LORD identifies "the people whom I have formed for myself" as those who are "called by my name, and whom I have created for my glory" (v. 6). In Daniel 9:19 "Your city and your people" falls in immediate proximity to "your name" (v. 18).

As we have seen, the use of "name" means much more than a mere label. It denotes who someone is by way of what someone does, and what someone does by way of what someone is. It is no less the case for the triune God. In the case of who God is and what he does for his people, AIRO carries with it that which only can apply to the Deity, as we have seen in more than a few biblical verses with the divine use of "name." In Matthew 28:19 we have the one divine name—the singular authority, identity, reputation, ownership—of the distinct divine persons of the Father and the Son and the Holy Spirit. Notice that in Matthew 28:19 Jesus and the Holy Spirit share in AIRO with the Father! For this reason among others we confess with the church throughout the centuries that the one God (the one with divine authority, identity, reputation, and ownership) is the Father and the Son and the Holy Spirit.

### More on 28:19–20

The Holy Trinity comes to us in the context of evangelism and discipleship. As mentioned in the Introduction, the church must not lose sight of this. In other words, the revealing of himself in the

---

5. The New Testament often applies to Jesus that which applies to the LORD (Yahweh). As a cross reference to Acts 9:15, see Exodus 9:16.

context of AIRO is also the revealing of himself in the context of giving himself for the salvation of the nations. If one *is* as one *does*, the triune God in his very being is "missionary"; that is, giving himself for humanity to believe in him and, through those who believe, lead others to himself in the person of the Lord Jesus Christ.

At the end of the Gospel of Matthew the Lord Jesus makes a stupendous claim: "I am with you always" (28:20). With the divine presence of Jesus the divine presence of the Father and the Holy Spirit are a reality in real time and space. Thus the rite of baptism of which we partake is not only something performed *toward* the triune God in external fashion, but also *with* the triune God by the divine presence of Jesus, and in communion with God the Holy Spirit. With Jesus the error of "great gulf" theology is smashed.

As an additional reality, in Matthew 28:19 baptism signifies that we have entered into the real and present authority, identity, reputation, and ownership (AIRO) "of the Father and the Son and the Holy Spirit." The act of baptism is more than just an act done externally toward the triune God and therefore apart from the triune God. It entails being performed in his presence. Moreover, baptism signifies that as servants we have entered into the name of the triune God, having done so on the objective ground of the substitutionary life and death of Christ. Baptism marks us as his servants who identify with and have entered into his life and his death on the cross. I'll explain briefly.

- *Into his authority.* For example, we share in the authority of Christ (Eph 2:6; Luke 10:17; Acts 4:7–10).

- *Into his identity.* Through functioning as and being the "Body of Christ" (1 Cor 12:27). Sharing in the sufferings of Christ and being crucified with Christ (2 Cor 1:5; Gal 2:20).

- *Into his reputation.* Through being followers of Christ and fellow heirs with Christ; suffering with him and later being glorified with him (Rom 8:17).

- *Into his ownership of us.* Like Paul, we are servants of Jesus (Rom 1:1). Also, the LORD says to his covenant people, "You are mine" (Isa 43:1).

21

AIRO evidences an *actual* sharing in the life of the triune God. The apostle Peter in 2 Peter 1:4 tells us that believers are "participants [or 'fellowshipers'] in the divine nature." The Greek word for "participants" is *koinonoi*. I think you might recognize this word being quite similar to "koinonia." *Koinonia* is "fellowship." Christians, by the indwelling grace of the Holy Spirit, participate in the life of the Holy Trinity by being holy (see the subsequent verses in 2 Peter 1 for what holiness looks like).

Because the doctrine of the Trinity ultimately must be understood and articulated in the context of the history of salvation, Jesus locates the triune name in the context of making disciples of all nations. Thus, one way in which we participate in the life of the triune God is (again, by the enabling presence of the Holy Spirit) by making disciples, baptizing them, and teaching them. Remember the Nicene Creed: Jesus came "for us and for our salvation." He comes for the salvation of the nations, and we, being in him, participate with him in the purpose of his coming.

## To Us and for Us

The Holy Trinity is not only revealed *to* us, but also *for* us. The triune God is revealed to us and for us in God the Son, the Lord Jesus, in actual history in a certain place, in and among a certain people—the nation of Israel. This is why the Nicene Creed mentions that Jesus "for us and for our salvation came down from heaven." He has come that we might have life, and have it more abundantly (John 10:10).

With the person of Jesus we know that the Holy Trinity is for us and gives himself to us. Through Jesus we know God the Father in communion with God the Holy Spirit. Thus, our knowing of the Trinity is not knowledge where our minds and thoughts travel, so to speak, to some God far away from us. Rather, the Holy Trinity is *really* present with us in Christ in the indwelling of the Holy Spirit. While we in worshipful adoration acknowledge the triune God's transcendence, we at the same time in worshipful adoration confess his real presence with us and in us by virtue of the real concrete historical appearance of the Son, through whom we are given the Spirit.

## Two Very Important Words

*Homo-ousios* and *peri-choresis*[6] are two words that can help us to see what is essential to proper understanding of the Holy Trinity, and thus to proper worship of the Holy Trinity. The former was especially emphasized in the early church during the Nicene and post-Nicene period (AD 325 and following). During this period these two words and the meaning behind them provided the ground necessary to combatting Arianism and provided the rich ground upon which Christian theology rests.

*Homo-ousios* is the Greek word meaning "[of the] same being/substance/nature/essence." This word was employed at the Council of Nicaea to convey that Jesus shares with the Father the same being or nature. The clue we receive for the doctrine of *homo-ousios* between the Father and the Son comes from John 1:1c: "The Word *was God.*" I will have much more to say on this in the chapter on the Son, but for now note that these words of John (under the inspiration of God the Holy Spirit) instruct us that the Son, here the eternal Logos of the Father, shares in the divine being with his Father. Of course, we must include the Holy Spirit as *homo-ousios* with the Son and the Father, as did the early church theologians, for in the Scripture, as we have seen in the "Basics" section, the Spirit is God. In the Gospel of John, Jesus instructs his disciples that he will send "another Helper"[7] (John 14:16), implying another *of the same kind*, in part because the ministry of the Holy Spirit is characteristic only of the Deity (John 14–16).

*Peri-choresis* refers to the "mutual indwelling" of the three divine persons, that the three persons of the Trinity eternally

---

6. Throughout this book, whenever I say the Father is called God, the Son is called God, and the Holy Spirit is called God; or whenever I say that the Father and the Son and the Holy Spirit are one God (or the one being), I do so with the implied understanding of *homo-ousios* and *peri-choresis*.

7. Or advocate, intercessor.

mutually indwell each other in self-giving love. Yet, though there is mutual indwelling, the distinctness of the persons must at the same time be confessed. The Gospel of John provides the teaching of *peri-choresis*. In John 17 Jesus states, "You, Father, *are* in me and I in you" (v. 21); "I am in the Father and the Father is in me" (John 14:11). As was the case with *homo-ousios* between the Father and the Son, with the *peri-choresis* of the Father and the Son we must add the Holy Spirit as indwelling the Father and the Son, just as the Father and the Son indwell the Holy Spirit.

Have we given much thought to how the three persons are "one"? Of crucial importance now is what follows theologically and logically on the heels of *homo-ousios* and *peri-choresis*. The reality of *homo-ousios* and *peri-choresis* of the Holy Trinity signals to us the *personal singular* triune being of the Father and the Son and the Holy Spirit. The doctrine of *peri-choresis* is essential to seeing the three distinct persons as *one* personal divine being. While the three divine persons are *homo-ousios*, they also indwell (*peri-choresis*) each other in their *homo-ousios* relationship, and therefore *are* the *one* personal and holy triune being (God). *Peri-choresis* and *homo-ousios* are for that very reason essential to understanding that the three distinct persons are one personal divine being. Because of this singular personal dynamic (with both *peri-choresis* and *homo-ousios*), we refer to the Holy Trinity in the singular because of their distinctly personal *peri-choretic* and *homo-ousial* dynamic. To put it another way, the three distinct persons who are *homo-ousios* indwell each other and in this way constitute the one personal being—the triune God who is the Father and the Son and the Holy Spirit.

The three divine persons of the Trinity possess will (1 Cor 12:11; Luke 22:42), intellect (Isa 1:18), and emotion (John 11:35; Eph 4:30). The persons of the Trinity cognitively and purposefully exhibit mutual love for one another in relationship, in divine freedom, and in very being, and therefore themselves are love coming to us and for us in Christ. The three divine persons in their intra-relations constitute what they *are*, ontologically, as the one God. For example, the Father as he relates to the Son and the Holy Spirit is why he is the Father; the Son as he relates to the Father and the

Holy Spirit is why he is Son; and the Holy Spirit as he relates to the Father and the Son is why he is the Holy Spirit.

## Worship and Proclamation

The church has with bowed head and bent knee expounded the doctrine of the Trinity in the inseparable context of adoration and proclamation, and with accuracy and precision.

Proper worship is expression in word and act that corresponds precisely to the revelation of the Holy Trinity revealed in Christ. Jesus was revealed "for us and for our salvation" so that we might know the Father in communion with the Holy Spirit. The doctrine of the Trinity should not be for us an exercise only in pronouncing the doctrine, but also the following: (1) Adoring the triune God as (A) the Father almighty, maker of heaven and earth; (B) the Son, the Lord Jesus, of one being (*homo-ousios*) with the Father, through whom all things were made, who came down from heaven for us and for our salvation; (C) the Holy Spirit, the Lord, the giver of life, who with the Father and the Son is worshiped and glorified.[8] (2) Proclaiming the Holy triune God, baptizing and discipling in and through and with him those who by the grace of the Holy Spirit come to know the Lord Jesus and God the Father.

## Analogies for the Trinity

My advice? Be careful. Before we get to analogies, here is a brief description of the heresies that deny the Trinity.

1. *Unitarianism.* A unitarian view of God postulates that only one person (usually the Father) is God. The Son is not God and neither is the Holy Spirit. Arius of Alexandria taught a form of unitarianism, as does Islam (though the quranic Allah is not called the Father) and the Unitarian Universalist Association.

2. *Modalism.* There is one person (God) who reveals himself as the Father, then as the Son, then as the Holy Spirit. A modern-day

8. From the Nicene-Constantinopolitan Creed of AD 381.

expression of modalism is the United Pentecostal Church International.[9] With modalism the three persons do not exist simultaneously; only one person does. This one person takes on three manifestations or "modes" of operation of himself at different times: the Father becomes the Son, becomes the Holy Spirit. (Modalism is a form of unitarianism.)

3. *Tri-theism.* Simply put, three separate gods. Mormonism teaches that for this planet there are three separate gods—the Father, the Son, and the Holy Ghost—who are one in purpose.

Here are some popular analogies people use to illustrate the doctrine of the Trinity.

1. *The egg:* There is one egg with three parts—shell, albumen, yolk. The problem here is that using "parts" as an analogy infers separation[10] of the three persons of the Trinity so that there is no mutual indwelling (*peri-choresis*) and *homo-ousios*. With "parts" there is no trinitarian *homo-ousios* because one part of the egg does not really and relationally share in the nature of the other parts. The same can be said of the apple analogy. Also, "three parts of one pie" separates the pieces to the extent that there is no *peri-choresis* between the separate pieces. Further, these analogies suggest tri-theism.

2. "I am one person who is a husband and a father and a construction worker." You guessed it—modalism!

3. "Water is a single substance which is liquid that becomes ice and then becomes steam." Modalism again![11]

9. United Pentecostal Church International, "Our Beliefs."

10. "Separate parts" communicates no real *inter*-relations. "Distinct persons" guards against the erroneous view of separate parts, for unlike separate parts, "distinct persons" leaves room for oneness (*homo-ousios*) and mutual indwelling (*peri-choresis*).

11. Some pushback might occur here. One can rebut by calling upon the "triple-point" where liquid, ice, and steam can exist simultaneously. There indeed is a triple-point, but upon further investigation the analogy breaks down. The water starts as a liquid substance and (1) changes functionally

4. Take a look at the following diagram. Though helpful to explain some of the dynamics in articulating the doctrine of the Trinity, note that there is no explicit indication of *homo-ousios* and *peri-choresis*, the substantial oneness and mutual indwelling of the Father and the Son and the Holy Spirit.[12] With no *homo-ousios* and *peri-choresis* as additional concepts, we could be left to speculation as to how "God" is the personal triune being.[13]

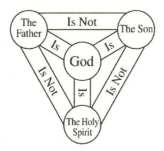

The next diagram[14] is well designed and quite helpful. First, both the circle and the lines should be seen as traveling in both directions (the circle around one way and the other; the lines back and forth). Second, of particular importance is the dynamic of "is in," which emphasizes *peri-choresis*. But in this diagram, as in the first, *homo-ousios* is explicitly missing. Perhaps three lines reading "is of the same essence with" connecting Father to Son and to Holy Spirit would round out the diagram nicely.

---

until it reaches a point where it appears as liquid, ice, and steam simultaneously; (2) the one substance of water that becomes liquid, ice, and steam at the triple-point does not evidence interpenetration of the three modes; they remain separate in the three phases or modes. This also suggests tritheism. As for 1, the substance changes in function and appearance from the original one substance (liquid). As for 2, there is in the fullest sense no *peri-choresis* between the liquid and the ice and the steam at the triple-point.

12. This chart is also used for the water analogy mentioned above.

13. Also, is "God" a fourth entity? Is "God" a "nature" or "essence"?

14. Taylor, "Using a Diagram."

So as for analogies, though they are well-meaning attempts to help us understand the Trinity, they all fall short of precise articulation.[15] We should seriously consider staying away from them and employ Scripture soundly as God the Holy Spirit communes in us and with us and leads us in his revelation of the Father and the Son to us.

## "Practical" vs. "Heady"?

"I'm not all into that heady stuff in theology. I am not a theologian. I want the practical." How do we respond to this statement? First, as soon as one starts talking about "God," one is a theologian (someone who gives a discourse on God). Second, dichotomizing between practical and heady (or "academic") is a false dichotomy, and some use it as an excuse not to engage in serious study. Let's explore this a bit more.

In order to be practical concerning anything, one has to think through the content at hand in order to determine the practical. Moreover, is not the very act of knowing about something

---

15. We can employ precise language while still remaining unable fully to comprehend. Put another way, we may still use the language of *homo-ousios* and *peri-choresis* even though we cannot plumb the full depths of the reality to which these words point.

"practical"? Those who only want the practical do not realize how practical it is first to know what it is they are being practical about! Let's apply this to theology. Is it not practical to know (by being a theologian) the triune God as he reveals himself? Now the question: How do we "practically" know the Holy Trinity? Practical knowledge and relationship with the triune God occurs by his communing-with-us grace and through the study of his word in prayerful, worshipful meditation upon him through the Scriptures, and with precise articulation of trinitarian doctrine (yes, even with some of the key words of the early church). That by itself is "practical" and at the same time fosters an ongoing and deepening relationship with the triune God. This is only possible with practical deep study of the word of the triune God as we commune with him in Christ. This characterizes the life of a Christian by the powerful indwelling presence of God the Holy Spirit. When it comes to knowing the Holy Trinity, all of the above is "practical."

One last word. Have we not often heard that we need to make Jesus (or, more frequently used, the gospel) "relevant" to others? What about making others relevant to Jesus? After all, Jesus is the most relevant and practical person (with the Father and the Holy Spirit) in this world. He, the blessed Son of God the Father, took on our humanity and in himself made that humanity holy, so that by grace through faith in him we would participate in his humanity, and through that be acceptable to the Father. To be relevant to Jesus is to be conformed to his image (Rom 8:29). To be relevant to Jesus is to be conformed to his death (Phil 3:10). To be relevant to Jesus is to "count all things to be loss in view of the surpassing value of knowing Christ Jesus my Lord" (Phil 3:8).

By the grace of the Holy Spirit, let's strive to make others relevant to Jesus, to be in relationship with Jesus, to the glory of the Father and the Holy Spirit.

As the next three chapters on the Father, the Son, and the Holy Spirit unfold, the distinctness of the three divine persons and their oneness in personal being (one God) will become more vivid. For now, let's remember that the Holy Trinity *is* three distinct persons as the one personal being of God. Further, let's remember that the triune God is revealed *to* us and *for* us and for our salvation in real space and time—in history—in the most profound sense[16] through the incarnation of the Lord Jesus Christ. Finally, remember to use your predicates!

# Discussion

1. Articulate some ways in which the triune God is *for* us. Use your predicates as you speak or meditate.

2. With worshipful acknowledgement to and adoration of the triune God, how might your knowing that he is *really* present *with* us affect your posture during baptisms and communion services?

3. What do *homo-ousios* and *peri-choresis* mean? Utilizing *homo-ousios* and/or *peri-choresis*, expound upon the following: the incarnation and virgin birth; Jesus as the only way to come to the Father; the ministry of Jesus, the Holy Spirit, or the Father; being born again; the sacrament of communion; the sacrament of baptism (in the latter two especially, don't forget the *real* presence of the Son [Matt 28:20] and the Holy Spirit [1 Cor 3:16; 6:19]).

4. Regarding analogies for the Trinity, would you use them or not? Why? Why not?

---

16. "In the most profound sense" because in the Old Testament the triune God was present with the covenant people of Israel, though not through the incarnation. That the triune God is acting in the Old Testament will become evident as we progress through the chapters that follow.

# CHAPTER 2

# *God the Father*

This chapter is the first of three chapters on each person of the Trinity. Through the revelation to us of the three divine persons, we through faith come to know God as Trinity and the Trinity as God.

## The Basics

Here we study Patrology.

Remember that God the Father is eternally Father in relation to God the Son and God the Holy Spirit. This relation eternally is one of *homo-ousios* and *peri-choresis*.

Throughout the Bible, there is a person called the Father and he is called God. For example, in 2 Peter 1:17 we read of "God the Father." In Isaiah 64:8 the people of Israel state, "LORD, you are our Father." Jesus specifically calls his God "Father" (for example, John 17:1). The Father is traditionally called the "first person of the Trinity." However, note carefully that this phrase should in no way be interpreted as "first to exist." All three distinct persons of the Trinity are *eternal*, sharing the same essence (*homo-ousios*) as the one personal being, or God. Think about it. The doctrine of *homo-ousios* forbids any idea of a chronological order of coming into existence as pertains to the Father, the Logos, and the Holy Spirit.

31

One reason the church traditionally affirms the order of "Father, Son, and Holy Spirit" is that with the conception of Jesus in the unfolding of the story of the Gospels, the Father sends the Son (John 3:16–17) who sends the Holy Spirit (John 16:7).[1]

As stated above, the Father is Father in eternal relation to the Son and the Spirit. For example, the Son in communion with the Holy Spirit reveals the Father (John 1:18). So we must never speak of God the Father with a mindset of separation between the Father and the Son and the Holy Spirit.

## What Is the Father Like?

How do we know what the Father is like? First, the Father is revealed as Father in the eternal Trinity. In the Introduction I mentioned that all theology takes place in the life of the triune God. Here is a sample of how that looks.

Let's start with Jesus in the context of trinitarian theology. Jesus, having been sent by the Father in communion with the Holy Spirit, has revealed the Father. John 1:18 reads, "No one has seen God[2] at any time; the only begotten, God,[3] who is in the bosom of the Father, he has explained him" (my translation). "Explained him." Jesus in his life and ministry explains the Father to us. So how do we know what the Father is like? We look at Jesus—what he said and what he did in the power of the Holy Spirit. Because Jesus is compassionate, loving, judge, and divine (to name a few characteristics), we know that the Father is compassionate, loving,

1. Though one can put it this simply, note carefully that there is a wider theological issue at stake. From whom does the Holy Spirit come (or "proceed")? In other words, who sends the Holy Spirit? The Father alone? The Father *and* the Son? When we think about answers to these questions, we must keep the doctrines of *homo-ousios* and *peri-choresis* in mind. Perhaps the best way to answer is to confess that the Holy Spirit proceeds *from* the Father *through* the Son, and *by* the Son *from* the Father (see Torrance, *Christian Doctrine*, 129). This would be a way forward to uniting the Western and Eastern traditions on this highly divisive matter. See the Glossary, "Filioque."

2. Here the Father. See John 6:46.

3. Here the Son. See John 1:1,14.

judge, and divine. In this way, we worship the Father and honor him by ascribing to him what we see when we look at Jesus.

But when you look at Jesus to see what God the Father is like, be careful to note that Jesus is *not* the Father. Athanasius once stated, "And so, since they are one, and the Godhead itself one, the same things are said of the Son, which are said of the Father, except His being said to be Father."[4] As we have seen in Chapter 1, there are three distinct persons of the Trinity who are such simultaneously. As we saw above, the Father sends the Son who sends the Holy Spirit (John 3:16–17; 16:7). This strongly implies three distinct persons.[5] Yet, in the act of sending, each of the three persons do not act alone but in unity. To send someone is to be distinct from that someone. Also, consider that three distinct persons of the Trinity are present when Jesus is baptized (Matt 3:16–17; 2 Pet 1:17).

## The Lord's Prayer

In addition to Jesus himself being the explanation of the Father and the one who reveals the Father (John 1:18), Jesus teaches us his prayer to the Father, which we pray with him to the Father. Let's look at the words of the prayer (Matt 6:9–13) and draw some conclusions that pertain to God the Father; and with Jesus and in communion with God the Holy Spirit, let's engage in worshipful adoration of the Father.

### Our Father who is in heaven

God the Father is first and foremost the Father of Jesus. Because Christians are "in Jesus" by grace through faith and are blessed with the indwelling of God the Holy Spirit, we pray with Jesus to "our Father." Our Father is "in heaven," here in part meaning that

4. Athanasius, *Against the Arians*, 3.4.

5. Moreover, and for example, Jesus prays *to* the Father, demonstrating that there are two distinct persons.

God the Father (with Jesus and the Holy Spirit) is transcendent over all.

## Let your name be sanctified

Popularly it is "hallowed be your name." The Father's name is to be "sanctified" or "set apart" or seen as "holy." Perhaps all three of these apply at once! The sense is, "Let your name be sanctified/set apart/be holy." As we have seen in the previous chapter, there is much to the meaning of "name" (remember AIRO?). The Father's authority, identity, reputation, and ownership of us should be set apart by us; in other words, as his children we need to acknowledge the uniqueness and absolute holiness of the Father in his acts, and worship him accordingly.

## Let your kingdom come

"Please, Father, let your kingdom come."

Jesus here refers to the throne of the Father, where he rules over all the created universe as sovereign. This includes specifically the earth. Jesus as the obedient Son of the Father prays with his followers that his Father's kingdom will come in all its glory and fullness.

With the coming of his Son, the kingdom more profoundly has come. But even though the kingdom of God the Father is in our midst (Luke 17:21), all creation remains under slavery to corruption and waits for the Lord to free it (Rom 8:20–21). Jesus leads us in prayer for this moment to become a reality.

The coming of the Lord Jesus is a foretaste of what is to come! His life and the miracles he did are a reality of the inaugurated kingdom of the Father and a pointer to the coming of his kingdom in all its fullness (Dan 7:14), which is the new heaven and the new earth. This is the new Jerusalem coming down from heaven from God the Father. There God the Father will dwell with us (Rev 21:1–4), and we will dwell with him everlastingly.

## Let your will be done

We pray with Jesus, "Father, . . . let your will be done." In all persecutions we face with Jesus as we live in him, we pray God the Father's will be done, for his will is perfect and right and true, and his kingdom *will* come. Jesus modeled this for his disciples before his crucifixion (Luke 22:42). He always, by the indwelling of the Holy Spirit within him, relied upon and did the will of his Father. And he did this *for* us, that in him we might join in his sufferings, staying true to him in the bold proclamation of his gospel as his kingdom invades the kingdoms of this world. Only by the indwelling and enabling grace of God the Holy Spirit, as we participate in Jesus, can we fulfill the will of the Father.

## On earth as it is in heaven

There are several options for meaning here. One is that as the name of the Father is set apart in heaven, so let it be on earth; as the Father's kingdom is in heaven, so let it be on earth; and as the Father's will is done in heaven, so may it be done on earth. As the last Adam and himself the true Israel, Jesus the obedient servant leads us in calling upon his Father's will to be done on earth even as it is in heaven. This is what we should pray in humility to God the Father as Jesus prays with us in communion with the Holy Spirit.

## Give us this day our daily bread

God the Father is provider. He cares for his children in his Son. We are to pray that the Father will supply "this day" our food, which sustains us. Expanding this, it is wonderful to ask the Father, in the name of Jesus, to supply us this day all our needs as we go forward with Jesus in his truth to make disciples of all nations.

*And forgive us our debts,*[6] *as we have forgiven our debtors*

God the Father is not only provider, he is also forgiver. Translations are several when it comes to whether we translate as "debts," "sins," "trespasses," "something owed," or "moral faults." The gist here is not to be a hypocrite. Our Father always is willing to forgive us, but if we hold something against others, we should not expect our Father to forgive us. The Father is the righteous judge and will discipline us. As we forgive, so should we also expect to be forgiven (Matt 6:14–15).

*And lead us not into temptation, but deliver us from the evil one*

We can translate here as "may you not lead us into temptation, but deliver us from the evil one." This is a very difficult verse to understand because "How can God lead us into temptation?" Interpretations are many. I shall offer one: "Please do not lead us into temptation."

Jesus himself must be the center in which we understand this, and we must remember two things: (1) Jesus came for us; and (2) we live *in* him and are crucified with him. Paul sums up points (1) and (2): "I have been crucified with Christ . . . who loved me and gave himself up for me" (Gal 2:20).

It is interesting that just two chapters earlier Jesus is led by God the Holy Spirit into the wilderness to be tempted by the devil (Matt 4:1). Moreover, Hebrews 4:15 tells us that he was tempted just as we are (yet, of course, without sin). Further, Jesus in Matthew 26:39 prays to the Father that his cup of suffering might be taken away. Yet he prays, "not as I will, but as you *will*."

Therefore, we first should understand "lead us not into temptation but deliver us from the evil one" as a prayer to the Father in full awareness that Jesus was led to temptation and suffering for us

---

6. Jesus praying this part of the prayer with us does not mean that he joins us as a sinner. Rather, Jesus as our great high priest and mediator takes our prayer of confession and presents it to the Father.

under the sovereign will and good purpose of his Father (cf. Heb 2:9–10).

Second, since we live in Jesus and he in us, and, following Paul, we have been crucified with Christ, just like him we will be led to be tempted and persecuted, and may even be called to die for his sake, to the glory of the Father and in the Holy Spirit. Yet, we with Jesus as the obedient servant of the Father, and in our situations of suffering for his sake and for his gospel, call upon the Father to deliver us from the evil one.

So Jesus did it *for* us in the most perfect way, resisting temptations brought to him by Satan when God the Holy Spirit led him into the wilderness. Like him and in him as true humanity, we plead with the Father not to bring us into trials and temptations; but when by his good and perfect will the Father does lead us that way (for our sake; cf. Jas 1:2–4), like Jesus and with Jesus we ask the Father to deliver us from the evil one.

*For yours is the kingdom and the power*
*and the glory forever. Amen*

We pray the above to God the Father because the kingdom belongs to him. To him belongs all power. To him all glory is to be given. We, like Jesus and in Jesus and with Jesus, are to trust the Father.

As we pray this prayer, remember to be mindful that our prayer takes place *within the life of the triune God*—the Father and the Son and the Holy Spirit. Additionally, we pray *to* the Father *through* and *in* and *with* the Son *in communion with* the Holy Spirit. "With" Jesus is most important here, for Jesus as our great high priest and mediator takes our prayer and perfectly presents it to the Father on our behalf.

## Discussion

1. What is the Father like? Look at some descriptions, words, and actions of Jesus and list them. Keep in mind, though, that whatever is said of Jesus is said of the Father, *except Father!*

2. Can you think of anything else you might know about the Father as you meditate on the Lord's prayer? Based on this, what will be some of the things you pay attention to in worship?

3. Now that you have addressed the above, use precise phrases in worshipful adoration of the Father (try to articulate your worship language in the context of the Trinity).

## Beyond the Basics

In our "Basics" section on patrology we looked at what the Father is like. When we look at Jesus, who is compassionate, loving, judge, and fully divine, because of *homo-ousios* and *peri-choresis* we should express the same of the Father in worship. With the Lord's Prayer, Jesus himself prays with us and in that prayer expresses some of what the Father is: one whose name (AIRO) should be set apart as holy; provider; protector; king, whose kingdom will one day fully be established; and one whose will we should strive to seek with the enabling grace of the Holy Spirit.

The triune God names himself as Father, Son, and Holy Spirit. We therefore confess and worship the triune God as such, and confess and worship the Father as he is and as he has revealed himself to us in Christ. We cannot confess God as Father without confessing his Son as Son; and this we can only do in communion with God the Holy Spirit.

We read in John 1:18 that the only begotten God, the Lord Jesus, is "in the bosom of the Father." This means that Jesus eternally possesses a unique Sonship with the Father (whereas Christians are those who are *adopted* by the Father [Eph 1:5; Gal 4:5]). Thus it is in the context of God the Father that we worship God the

Son; and in worshiping Jesus as God the Son we equally honor the Father (John 5:23).

## An Exercise in Predicates

In the New Testament, "God" often (not always [John 20:28, for example]) refers to the Father. In the Old and New Testaments we see many instances of "God" appearing without any predicate.[7] So how do we determine proper predicates. It is not easy at first, but here are three examples with which to practice.

We'll start with a hard one first![8]

Genesis 1:1 reads, "In the beginning God created the heavens and the earth." What is the predicate for "God" here?

In verse 2 we see that "the Spirit of God was moving over the surface of the waters." This makes it easy to see that "God" in these two verses is the Father. This is why, in part, the Nicene Creed and the Nicene-Constantinopolitan Creed confess God the Father as "maker of heaven and earth."

Second, let's do some theology. What about the Holy Trinity, the triune God? Since we know theologically that "God" also refers to the Trinity, we can look at Genesis 1:1–3 to see if the Father and the Son and the Holy Spirit are the one creator of the heavens and the earth (the doctrine of *homo-ousios* leads us to this conclusion!). The Holy Spirit is involved in the creation of all things, for we read that the Spirit of the Father was moving over the surface of the waters. Now look at verses 3, 6, 9, 14, 20, 24, 26, and 29: "Then God said . . ." What of this? The Father always speaks through his Word. Isn't it interesting that in John's Gospel, the very first verse mentions "the Word" (Logos) "In the beginning"? John is setting the first verse of his Gospel in the context of the creation of all

---

7. Oftentimes it is difficult to ascertain predicates. See, for example, various Psalms where the Hebrew *elohim*, translated "God," is used. This does not necessarily mean, however, that scripture is ambiguous. The difficulty is on our end. We thus must do our best to discern.

8. There are a few other ways to interpret what is meant by "God" in Genesis 1. Above, I offer one interpretation among other options.

things in Genesis 1. It is no far stretch at all, therefore, to see in Genesis 1 the Father in intimate union with his Son, the pre-incarnate Christ, bring all things into existence. Further, theologically, we see in John 1:3 that "All things came into being through him," the pre-incarnate Word of the Father.

In Genesis 1:26 we read, "Let *us* . . ." Here the Father includes with himself the Son (the Word) and the Spirit in the making of humanity "in *our* image, according to *our* likeness." Genesis 1:27 then reads, "So God created man in his own image." The predicate here for God is Father,[9] but to be created in the image of the Father is to be created in the image of the Father and the Son and the Holy Spirit (v. 26, "us"), as *homo-ousios* communicates. Take a moment to think about *homo-ousios* in Genesis 1:26–27.

In the above, we first determined the proper predicate for "God" in Genesis 1. We then we concluded theologically that in Genesis 1 the Holy Trinity is involved in creating all things. This is an example of the doctrine of creation being set squarely in the life of the Holy Trinity.

Now for a few examples of predicates from the New Testament.

In John 4:24, Jesus states, "God is spirit, and those who worship him must worship in spirit and truth." What is the predicate here for "God"? See verse 23: "true worshipers will worship the Father in spirit and truth." So the predicate for "God" here is the Father.

How about Paul's letters? Let's look at 1 Corinthians 10:31: "Whether you eat or drink, or whatever you do, do all things for the glory of God." What is the predicate for "God" here? In the introductions to many letters and books of the New Testament, we have at the beginning of them phrases such as "God our Father," "the God and Father," or "God the Father." So, to help us determine the predicate for "God" in 1 Corinthians 10:31, we look at the very

---

9. This mention of God could refer to the Trinity, since "our image" in verse 26 synonymously parallels "his image" in verse 27. I am familiar with the interpretations of "our" as the heavenly court or as a royal "we," but find them to be unacceptable because of the synonymous parallel here between "our" and "God" in light of the whole context of Genesis 1, where God and his Word and the Holy Spirit set the context in the early verses.

beginning of 1 Corinthians. Look at 1:3, where we read "God our Father." Thus, we can conclude that the predicate for "God" in 10:31 is the Father.

Determining proper predicates is important. It guards against thinking of an abstract, useless, and meaningless word ("God" can be an empty slogan) and at the same time helps listeners understand properly which person of the Trinity is the referent. Further, we should place our theologizing within the life of the Trinity. In other words, our theology is first trinitarian at its base, and therefore trinitarian in the way we "speak."[10]

The Nicene-Constantinopolitan Creed (and the Nicene Creed) begins with "We believe in one God the Father Almighty, maker of heaven and earth." Predicates right away ("the Father almighty")! Notice two things here.

First, God is called Father. That means that his identity is placed squarely in the context of his Son, the Lord Jesus who is God the Son; for the Father cannot be Father except in (eternal) relation with his Son.

Second, the very first sentence of the creed begins this way (showing that he is Father in relation to his Son) because the theologians crafting the creed were careful not to read into "God" some sort of abstract, meaningless notion. We read here of a concrete identity of God *as Father* even before we read "maker of heaven and earth." Athanasius long ago stated, "It would be more godly and true to signify God from the Son and call him Father, than to name God from his works alone and call him Unoriginate." The Father, then, is *specifically* God the Father almighty, maker of heaven and earth, who is the Father of our Lord Jesus Christ. To worship in this theological posture is GAWP.

---

10. See Torrance, *Ground and Grammar*. By "ground" Torrance means that the Trinity is the foundation upon which Christian doctrine rests. By "grammar" Torrance means that our theological reflections and articulations must find their center in, and be controlled by, the triune God and his revelation to us and for us in Jesus Christ.

## The Father in the Son

I shall address the doctrine of the Son in the Father in this section. We will also look at the Father being in the Son.

In Chapter 1, I brought attention to the doctrine of *peri-choresis*, that the Father and the Son and the Holy Spirit mutually indwell each other. That the Father is *in* the Son is one of the most difficult biblical truths to comprehend. We of course are unable to comprehend this doctrine fully, and therefore our language and understanding will fall far short of exhausting the relationship between God the Father and God the Son, but we surely can grasp something of it! The Gospel of John helps us here, as we, in communion with God the Holy Spirit, meditate on what the Spirit has revealed to us through this great apostle.[11]

We first take a clue from John 1:1, where we read that "the Word was God." The Word, who is God the Son and the pre-incarnate Christ, shares with the Father the same being. This equality of being between the Father and the Son (and of course the Holy Spirit) led the theologians of the Nicene Creed to employ the word *homo-ousios* (one essence/being) when describing the relationship of the Son to the Father ("one being with the Father"). So, note that according to John, the Father and the Son share the same essence that is *theos*.

In addition to asserting right from the outset the *homo-ousios* between the Father and the Son (John 1:1c), John in a later chapter recalls the words of the Lord Jesus in John 14:10: "I am in the Father and the Father is in me." In John 17:21 Jesus says, "You, Father, are in me and I in you." What does this mean? What is precisely the case here is *peri-choresis*. The Father is in the Son forever in perfect and undivided relationship of mutual indwelling. Yet, we must remember that although the Father is in the Son, this in no way blurs the distinction between the persons of the Father and the Son.

When we worshipfully meditate on the relationship between the distinct persons of the Father and the Son as one of *homo-ousios* and *peri-choresis*, we should be mindful that these two

---

11. Eastern traditions often use the phrase "St. John the Theologian."

realities are *dynamic* realities, that is, with them come both being *and* actions (doings) simultaneously (one is as one does). So we do well to recall the words of Athanasius as he instructs his readers in the context of the oneness of being: "There is nothing but the Father operates it through the Son."[12] So with these three notions—distinctness, *homo-ousios*, and *peri-choresis*—we know that what Jesus does, the Father does.[13] Further, these three doctrinal anchors enable us to grasp the truth that when God the Holy Spirit indwells Jesus and empowers his ministry, we have the incarnate reality of Jesus of Nazareth revealing the actions of the triune God in real time, in history. Take a moment to dwell on these three doctrines, asking yourself in their light how it is that what the Father does, Jesus does; and how it is that the words and acts of Jesus reveal the Holy Trinity.

## God the Father as Patriarch

God and Father reveals himself to the patriarchal society of the nation of Israel, and the nation gets its patriarchal structure due to God the Father eternally being Father. The nation of Israel is patriarchal precisely because God the Father is in himself Father.

In the Old Testament, Israel was tribal and patriarchal. "In a tribal society the family is, literally, the axis of the community."[14] In a patriarchal society, the patriarch of a family took the lead in running the "family compound." In turn, as the family grew too large (or if the patriarch died), members of the family formed patriarchal families themselves and formed a "clan" in interconnectedness with the original family. In time, many clans formed into tribes, which, collectively, became the nation of Israel.

Israelite patriarchs were central figures and responsible for the well-being of their families as they lived in their particular father's

12. Athanasius, *Against the Arians*, 3.12.

13. See John 5:17: "My Father is working until now, and I myself am working."

14. Richter, *Epic of Eden*, 25. This point and much of what follows is taken from Richter, especially pages 25–28.

house (family compound). According to Richter, the patriarch's responsibilities included the economic well-being of his family, enforcing law and justice, and caring for any in the family who were marginalized through poverty or death or war.[15] Moreover, "In extreme situations, [the patriarch] decided who lived and who died."[16] Finally, members of an Israelite family would *wholly* gather their identities in relation to the family to which they belonged, then to clan, then to tribe, and then to the nation[17] (a rather different picture compared to us in the West!).

From this brief survey of Israelite culture, many of the characteristics of patriarchs are reflected in the person of God the Father: provider; enforcing law; distributing justice; taking care of the widow and the orphan; and the fount of the identity of all family members.

## The "Family Compound" or "Father's House"

As mentioned above, the patriarch's family lived in the patriarch's "house" or "family compound." When in Israel, I visited the excavation of a family compound. Unfortunately, due to age, all that could be seen were the foundations of many "dwelling places" that collectively made up the family compound. It was fascinating to see! Immediately I recalled the words of the Lord Jesus from John 14:2 in a particular version of the Bible, "In my Father's house are many mansions" (KJV). To English readers, "mansions" communicates the idea of a huge house, instead of dwelling places within a father's family compound. "In my Father's family compound are many dwelling places" captures the sense quite vividly. As a Jew, Jesus knew this context well. The dwelling places Jesus saw and was familiar with became an illustration of what the new heaven and new earth, the new Jerusalem, would be like, and much more! There are going to be many "dwelling places" in the Father's new

15. Richter, *Epic of Eden*, 25.

16. Richter, *Epic of Eden*, 27.

17. Richter, *Epic of Eden*, 25–26.

heaven and earth, in his "compound" reserved for the saints who overcome, and we know this because the Lord Jesus said, "I go to prepare a place for you" (John 14:2)[18]

## Discussion

1. Read 2 Thessalonians 3:5. What is the proper predicate for "God" in that verse?

2. Employing the doctrines of *homo-ousios* and *peri-choresis* in the Gospel of John (1:1c and 14:10), interpret John 5:17, 23; 8:42; and 10:30.

---

18. The Father's place is also *his* place.

CHAPTER 3

# God the Son

The Son is Son always in relation to the Father and the Holy
Spirit. The relationship is eternally *homo-ousios* and *peri-choresis*. The doctrines of *homo-ousios* and *per-choresis*, from which
we must never turn away, compel us to worship the Trinity with
these dynamics in place. In this chapter we focus upon Jesus. Let's
begin!

## The Basics

Christology presents to us several profound truths as we plum-
met the depth of the Scriptures in their witness to the person of
God the Son, the Logos of God the Father. In this section we will
explore the pre-existence of God the Son, his incarnation among
us in history, and his resurrected and glorified existence in history
at the right hand of the Father.

## Fully God; Fully Man

Jesus is fully God and fully man. He is (*still* is!) God the Son and
fully human at the same time. Jesus possesses two natures as one
person. He possesses each nature in all its fullness. We will get to
the Scriptures soon, but for now let's consider the Council of Nicaea and the Council of Chalcedon. Regarding Jesus being fully

God, Nicaea uses the word *homo-ousios* to affirm that Jesus shares the *same being* with the Father. So with Nicaea the issue was the Son's relation to the Father, and the council confessed that Jesus was and is *fully God* by nature. With Chalcedon the issue in part was how Jesus's two natures (*theos* and humanity) related to each other. That council not only affirmed that Jesus was *homo-ousios* with the Father according to the deity, but also that he was and is *homo-ousios* with us according to his humanity. These two biblical teachings (one essence with the Father and one essence with us) involve a few categories we now explore.

## The Eternal Pre-existence of God the Son

The Word of God the Father, the Logos of John 1:1, is the pre-incarnate God the Son.

John 1:1 reads, "In the beginning was the Word [*logos*], and the Word was with God, and the Word was God." Let's take these three clauses separately and examine them briefly.

Clause A reads "In the beginning was the Word." Do those first three words sound familiar? Right, Genesis 1 and its opening words, "In the beginning . . ." Here in his Gospel, John is alerting us to something. It is as if he is shouting, "Readers, go to Genesis 1 for the context of what I am about to say!" So the scene is the time when all things were created, brought into existence by the triune God.

Clause B reads "and the Word was with God." With whom? "God." But this is not some ambiguous word. "God" here refers specifically to the Father. Why? Look at 1 John 1:1–2. John opens this letter with reference to "the Word of life" (cf. John 1:1, 4) who "was with the Father." First John 1:2 and its "was with the Father" is the same as John 1:1 and its "was with God." Thus, in John 1:1 "the Word was *with God*" means that the Word was *with the Father*.

Clause C reads "and the Word *was God*." Jehovah's Witnesses, in their denial of Jesus as God the Son,[1] sometimes like to chal-

---

1. Such a denial has eternal consequences: "Unless you believe that I am, you will die in your sins." Sadly, anyone who dies in denial that Jesus is God the

lenge Christians with this argument: "If Jesus is God, was he with himself"? Their argument seems very powerful. They say, "You believe the Word was God, and yet the Word was with God! Was he with himself? What a senseless thing to believe!" This is a great example of what it means to have our predicates in place and ready to go. If we simply let "God" in clause B remain without a predicate, confusion can arise. Therefore, it is vital that with clause B "God" is God the Father.

All well and good, so far. Clause B tells us that the Word, the pre-incarnate God the Son, was with the Father. But what about clause C, which reads "and the Word was God"? A great question to ask here is that if in clause B "God" refers to the Father, does "God" in clause C refer to the Father? NO! Here's why.

The apostle John, under the inspiration of God the Holy Spirit, knew what he was doing! We will delve deeper into this in "Beyond the Basics," but basically here is what John is doing. John is teaching us that not only is God the Son eternally "with" the Father (clause B), he also shares in the same being with the Father (clause C). In short, in clause C John is *not* saying that Jesus is the Father but that Jesus, in all his being as God the Son, is *theos* by nature. What we have to keep in mind with "God" in clauses B and C, is that in clause B "God" refers to the Father, while in clause C "God" is used differently, that is, used to describe the *nature* of the Son—he is by nature *theos*.

How about that little verb "was" in all three clauses? That little verb is explosive with meaning! It means "eternally was." The Son eternally "was" when all things were created, eternally "was" with the Father, and eternally "was" God by nature. This is why Christians believe that God the Son eternally pre-existed[2] (that is, "was" prior to his incarnation).

---

Son and the "I AM" will spend eternity outside the presence of the triune God. This is eternal punishment, "the lake of fire" (Rev 20:15).

2. Inserting "eternally" into our confession of the pre-existence of Christ is necessary to distinguish biblical teaching from heresy. For example, Mormons and Jehovah's Witnesses say they believe in the pre-existence of Jesus. Imagine having a conversation with them and they nodding their heads up and down because we use the word "pre-existence" with no qualifier? However, once we

Coming round now, let me paraphrase John 1:1: In the beginning, when everything was created, God the Son, the pre-incarnate Word, eternally was. And this eternal God the Son was eternally with the Father. And what the Father eternally is by nature, the Son also is eternally by nature—he shares in the same being with the Father.

One more verse for the eternal pre-existence of Jesus. In John 8:58 Jesus makes the astounding claim, "before Abraham was born, *I am*." This affirms the eternal pre-existence of God the Son, who is the "Word" in John 1:1. Cross-reference this "I am" of Jesus with the claim of Yahweh (LORD) in Exodus 3:14. God (Hebrew *elohim*) commissions Moses to go to Egypt to command Pharaoh to let the people of Israel go. Moses then asks about what he should say when he goes to the sons of Israel and they ask for God's name. Yahweh says, "I AM WHO I AM." Jesus in John 8:58 claims that he is the God and the LORD who identified himself to Moses as "I AM."[3] This phrase "I AM" means that Yahweh *is*. Simply yet profoundly, he *is*. He eternally is. So God the Word (the pre-incarnate Jesus) is "alive and well" in the Old Testament. As the eternally pre-incarnate God the Son he appeared to the saints of old. I shall have more on that later.

---

place the word "eternal" before "pre-existence," we distance ourselves from their false teachings. How so? Mormons define the pre-existence of Christ as follows: before he became a man, Jesus was the first-born spirit child of Heavenly Father and Heavenly Mother. Jesus did not eternally exist *as God*, but came into being, before his incarnation, as a spirit-child. Jehovah's Witnesses define the pre-existence of Christ in this way: before his incarnation, he was Michael the archangel, the first creature created directly by Jehovah. Thus, they say, Jesus pre-existed as Michael. To reiterate, in this inter-religious world it is not enough simply to state that Jesus pre-existed, but that Jesus *eternally* pre-existed.

3. This means that the predicate for "LORD" in Exodus 3 is the pre-incarnate Christ, the Logos of the Father. The pre-incarnate Christ as the predicate for LORD is found throughout the Old Testament. Determining the predicate for LORD in the Old Testament involves the cross-referencing of New Testament verses and passages with the Old Testament.

## The Incarnate Deity of Jesus

When he walked among people in New Testament times, Jesus himself was the incarnate Son of God the Father. He was God the Son. John 8:58, which we just looked at, also evidences Jesus's incarnate deity, for Jesus in his incarnate reality states, "I am." One more verse suffices to show that Jesus was God the Son incarnate. In John 20:28, Thomas makes what I consider the most concise and powerful confession for the incarnate deity of Jesus. When Jesus appears to his disciples after his bodily resurrection,[4] Thomas said to Jesus, "My Lord and my God!"

## Jesus as Fully Man

Christ is *incarnate* deity. He is God the Son "in the flesh"; God the Son *as human*. In John 1:14 we read that "the Word became flesh." The Logos of God the Father, the Word of God the Father, became a full human being. This does not mean that the Word *changed* to a man. It means that the Word, who eternally was with the Father and eternally was deity by nature (John 1:1), took to himself a full human nature to the extent that at the very moment of his conception in the womb of Mary he became (and still is) a human being.

Throughout his Gospel, John demonstrates what "became flesh" means. John teaches us that Jesus is human in the fullest sense: Jesus was deeply emotional and wept at the death of Lazarus (11:33–35), died a real death (19:33), and experienced great zeal for his Father's temple (2:14–18). In Luke we are told that Jesus was circumcised and presented to the Lord, as every firstborn male

---

4. "Resurrection" must also have a predicate: "bodily." Christ's resurrection was a *bodily* resurrection, not a resurrection merely of his spirit. Adding "bodily" before the word "resurrection" guards us against this false view. In my teaching experience I often have been asked the question, "Does Jesus still have a body?" Yes, he still has a body—he is, right now, fully man; a glorified and resurrected man. See 1 Timothy 2:5, where Paul states that there is one mediator between God the Father and humanity, *the man* Christ Jesus. Paul of course wrote this after Jesus's resurrection and ascension, which communicates that after his resurrection and ascension, Jesus is still a man.

was (2:21–23). "The child [Jesus] continued to grow and became strong, increasing in wisdom; and the grace of God [the Father] was upon him" (2:40). And, quite telling, like a human being Jesus "became twelve" and was obedient to his parents (2:51).

Rather than his deity overwhelming or stamping out his humanity, Jesus is truly human and truly man; he as one person possesses two natures.

## Discussion

1. Discuss or meditate upon what it looks like to worship Jesus. This will take some time, but try to do so (1) with the Trinity in mind, and (2) with your worship taking place within the life of the Trinity.

2. Dig deep and explain what it meant for Thomas to say to Jesus, "My Lord and my God" (John 20:28). In order to do this, call upon some of what John tells us earlier in his Gospel.

### Beyond the Basics

The Son is always the Son in relation to the Father and the Holy Spirit. The doctrine of *homo-ousios* compels us to think of him and to worship him in this way. In other words, we must think of the Son as he is Son in the Trinity.

### God and Man as One Person

The following chart explains three verses in John 1.

The section on John 1:1 contains three clauses, each clause having a transliteration (which gives you in English the pronunciation of the Greek words so you actually can pronounce John 1:1 in Greek!) on the top and a translation on the bottom (the same for John 1:3). Notes follow. The chart also contains a deep look into verses 3 and 14. The chart ends with a brief word on the Council of Chalcedon.

## John 1:1

> In the beginning was the Word, and the Word was with God, and the Word was God.

Clause A

| En | archē[5] | ēn | ho | logos |
|----|----------|-----|-----|-------|
| In | beginning | was | the | Word |

Notes. 1: *en archē* takes us back to Genesis 1:1, when all things were created. 2: Note the verb *ēn*, "was," which is a past tense continuous action verb, communicating "[eternally] was." This verb occurs three times in John 1:1. Also, this is a past tense verb of *eimi*, "I am." 3: "The Word" (Logos) is the pre-incarnate Jesus. 4: Thus, when all things were created, the Word always/eternally "was."

Clause B

| kai | ho | logos | ēn | pros | ton | theon |
|-----|-----|-------|-----|------|-----|-------|
| and | the | Word | was | with | the | God |

Notes. 1: The pre-incarnate Jesus eternally was "with the God." Who is "the God"? He is the Father. See 1 John 1:1–2, where we read about the "Word of life which was with the Father" (*pros ton patera*). 2: Thus, the pre-incarnate Jesus always was with the Father. 3: "With" (*pros*) denotes two distinct persons—the Son and the Father—who are eternally "with" each other.

Clause C

| kai | theos | ēn | ho | logos |
|-----|-------|-----|-----|-------|
| and | God | was | the | Word |

---

5. You can pronounce "ch" as "k" as in "kite." Whenever you see an "e" with a horizontal line over it, pronounce it as "a" as in "play." Thus pronounce this word like "are-kay." When you see "e" with no line over it, pronounce it as "e" as in "bet."

Notes. 1: "God" (*theos*) here does not refer to "the God" of clause B. In clause B *theon* refers to the Father. Here in clause C, *theos* has a different ending (*s*) than does *theon* (*n*) in clause B, so with *theon* referring to the Father in clause B, the Greek here in clause C has *theos* referring to the nature/essence/quality of "the Word" (who, again, is the pre-incarnate Jesus). 2: Thus, the pre-incarnate Jesus always was *theos* by nature. 3: John purposely leaves out "the" before *theos* in clause C (though he uses "the" in clause B). Why? So as to keep readers from thinking the Word was/is the Father. 4: As regards clauses B and C, in clause B the eternal ("was") distinction of the persons of the Father and the Son is evidenced by "with" (*pros*), and in clause C the Son is *theos* and so is eternally ("was") of the same being with the Father.

## John 1:3

| *Panta* | *di'* | *autou* | *egeneto* |
|---------|-------|---------|-----------|
| All things | through | him | became |

| *kai* | *choris*[6] | *autou* | *egeneto* | *oude* | *hen* | *ho* | *gegonen* |
|-------|-----------|---------|-----------|--------|-------|------|-----------|
| and | without | him | became | not | one | that | was made |

Notes. 1: The "all things" are the things created in Genesis 1. 2: In the Greek translation of the Old Testament, which is called the LXX or Septuagint, in Genesis 1 the verb *egeneto* is used for all the things that "became." 3: See the distinction between the verbs *ēn* in John 1:1 and *egeneto* here. *Egeneto* denotes things that "became" at a point in time, whereas *ēn* (remember, this is the past tense verb of *eimi*, "I am") denotes "always was," eternally existing. So, all things *became*, but the Word *always was*. 4: The first eighteen verses of the Gospel of John are known as the prologue. In places in the rest of

---

6. Technically the "o" in this word should have a horizontal line over it. I leave it out here because it does not affect pronunciation. Some of the "o"s in the rest of this chart technically should have horizontal lines, but also have been left out.

the Gospel the themes of the first eighteen verses are fleshed out or illustrated. (For examples, see John 1:14 cf. 12:41; John 1:18 cf. 6:46.) In John 8:58 the verb distinction between *ēn* and *egeneto* is illustrated: "Before Abraham *became* [*genesthai* (related to *egeneto* of John 1:3)], I AM [*ego eimi*: I, I am]." 5: A theological paradigm: God is *I am/you are/he is*; creation is *to become*. In the LXX of Psalm 89:2 (English, 90:2) we read, "Before the mountains *to become* [*genēthēnai* (also related to *egeneto* of John 1:3)], *you are* [*su ei*]."

## John 1:14

> And the Word became [*egeneto*] flesh, and dwelt among us; and we saw his glory, glory as of the only *Son* from the Father, full of grace and truth.

"And the Word became [*egeneto*] flesh"

Note. Jesus's flesh (humanity) "became" (*egeneto*). His humanity had a beginning in time. His humanity is *not* eternal. (If his humanity were eternal, he would not be like we are in every respect and would therefore not be able to die for us [cf. Heb 2:14–17].)

"and dwelt [*eskēnosen*] among us; and we saw his glory"

Notes. We focus here on "dwelt" and "glory." 1: "Dwelt" is "divine presence" language. See 2 Samuel 7:6: "For I have not dwelt in a house since the day I brought up the sons of Israel from Egypt, even to this day; But I have been moving about in a tent, even in a tabernacle" (my translation). 2: See Exodus 40:34–35 for "dwelt" and "glory": "Then the cloud covered the tent of meeting, and the glory of the LORD filled the tabernacle [LXX *skēnē*]. And Moses was not able to enter the tent of meeting because the cloud had settled on it, and the glory of the LORD filled the tabernacle [*skēnē*]." 3: Tabernacle language applies to the LORD here in Exodus. Compare *skēnē* ("tabernacle") in Exodus with "dwelt [*eskēnosen*] among us" here in John 1:14. John says Jesus "tabernacled among us." John equates Jesus with the LORD of Exodus 40:34–35. 4: Glory language applies to the LORD in Exodus 40:34–35, and John applies this glory language to Jesus. 5. To sum up, with Jesus himself we have the divine presence and glory of God dwelling bodily.

"full of grace and truth"

Note: Exodus 34:6 "The LORD, the LORD God, compassionate and gracious, slow to anger, and full of grace and truth" (my translation). Once again John applies to Jesus that which only applies to the LORD in the Old Testament.

### The Testimony of the Bible and of the Creed of Chalcedon

> Jesus possesses two natures, divine and human, in union one with the other. Each nature is possessed in its fullness. The two natures are *united*, not mixed and not divided. Jesus is *homo-ousios* with the Father according to the Godhead, and *homo-ousios* with us according to the Manhood.

*Explanation*

Let's put some narration to the notes above, starting with John 1:1 and its three clauses.

"In the beginning" calls our attention to Genesis 1:1. This, says John, is the context. But notice the next three words: "was the Word." This seemingly little verb "was" is profound. That verb communicates to us that in the beginning, that is, when all things were created, the Word (the pre-incarnate Son of the Father) "was." He *always* was! There *never* was a time when he came into existence. He eternally was with the Father.

Clause B communicates that the Word *was* with the Father (cf. 1 John 1:1–2). There's that verb again. The Word eternally was (and is) with the Father. "With" is also important to note. We have two persons who are "with" each other, and therefore two *distinct* persons—the Father and the Son. We also have the beginnings of trinitarian theology—two distinct persons.

Clause C is very important in comparison to clause B. We see in clause B that there is the definite article "the" before "God." We also saw that " the God" in clause B refers to the Father. If "the God" in clause B refers to the Father, what would we have to conclude if in clause C John had included the definite article "the" before "God"? Put another way, if John said "and the Word was with the God, and the Word was the God," who would the Word be? The Word would be the Father. Therefore we would have to embrace the heresy of modalism, where Jesus is the Father. But John purposefully leaves out the definite article in clause C (he could have included it if he believed Jesus was the Father). He carefully and with precision lets us know that Jesus is *not* the Father. Instead, John communicates to us that not only was Jesus eternally "with" the Father (clause B) as a distinct person, but also that what the Father is in being, the Son is in being and shares with his Father that being.

Before we look at the relation between John 1:1 and John 1:3, I want to share a bit on the function of the first eighteen verses of John. The first eighteen verses are known as the prologue, which introduces the Gospel.

I grew up watching *Rudolph the Red-Nosed Reindeer*. Near the beginning of the show, the introductory music comes in. It is a medley of many of the songs, each in very short portion, introducing the tunes we will hear during this short animated movie. During the movie, the songs in the introductory overture are "fleshed out" in full.

Think of the prologue to the Gospel of John in the same way. There are introductory themes in the prologue that John will flesh out throughout the Gospel.

Here is an amazing example of the prologue of John (1:1–18) introducing a theme that is fleshed out later in the Gospel (details for which are in the notes for John 1:3 in the chart above). Though much of what follows was mentioned earlier, let's reexamine it, keeping in mind the paradigm of prologue and "fleshing out." In the prologue, compare *was* in John 1:1 with "became" in John 1:3. As mentioned in John 1:1, "was" is a past tense verb of "I am." But in 1:3 we read that all things "became." This theme of Jesus "was" and all things "became" is fleshed out for us in the words of Jesus in John 8:58: "Before Abraham to become, I AM." The contrast here recalls the contrast introduced by the verbs in John 1:1, 3. We therefore are compelled to conclude that Jesus is "I AM," but Abraham, just like "all things," became. As the eternal Son of God the Father, Jesus is *not* among the things created.[7]

Here are three more examples of how John fleshes out what is found in the prologue.

First, John 17:5. "And now you, Father, glorify me together with yourself, with the glory which I had with you before the world existed." This fleshes out John 1:14, which reads, "and we saw his glory." As we can see, John 17:5 inserts more content into the claim of 1:14.

Second and third, John 1:18: "No one has seen God at any time; the only begotten, God, who is in the bosom of the Father, he has explained *him*" (my translation). Who is the person that is represented in the first mention of "God," whom no one has seen at any time? John 6:46 answers this question. Jesus says, "Not that anyone has seen the Father." So Jesus himself furnishes for us the predicate for the first instance of "God" in John 1:18—the Father. Therefore when we read the phrase in John 1:18, we can supply the predicate in order to understand better the sense: "No one has seen God [the Father] at any time." Further along in the verse, John states that Jesus has "explained"[8] the Father. John later fleshes out this statement when he recalls Jesus's answer to Philip's request to "show us the Father." Jesus states, "The one who has seen me has seen the Father" (John 14:8–9).

---

7. As Jehovah's Witnesses and certain other pseudo-Christian religions would have us believe.

8. The Greek verb here is *exēgēsato*, for which we derive the word "exegesis," which means "to draw out [the meaning]." Jesus himself is the exegesis of the Father. This why Jesus answers Philip, saying "the one who has seen me has seen the Father" (John 14:8–9).

Now some thoughts on his full humanity (and more on his deity). For this we focus on John 1:14, outlined above in the chart.

We must confess that Jesus's humanity is humanity in the fullest sense (truly human; truly a man). He is "the man Christ Jesus" *right now* (1 Tim 2:5). We therefore must worship him as such, to the glory of God the Father and God the Holy Spirit. Because he "became flesh," that is, became a full human being, his humanity is a vicarious (substitutionary) humanity, from his conception in the womb of Mary to his ascension to the right hand of God the Father.[9] The Logos of God the Father took to himself a full human nature and became both God and man. From the moment of his conception in the womb of the virgin Mary by the agency of God the Holy Spirit,[10] Jesus began vicariously reconciling humanity to the Father as he lived in communion with the Father and the Holy Spirit. As such, Jesus as both God and man is the reconciling salvific movement of the triune God to humanity and humanity to the triune God.[11] His whole life is one of substitutionary atonement (reconciling), which culminates with his substitutionary death and resurrection and ascension for us and for our sake, to the glory of God the Father. All, then, who receive Jesus (John 1:12), all who confess him and call upon his name (Rom 10:9–13), will be saved.[12]

In John 1:14, Jesus "became flesh." This phrase is then fleshed out throughout the Gospel of John, and no one reading John can

9. Unfortunately, oftentimes (if not always) when we hear the words "vicarious" or, more usually, "substitutionary," our thoughts are drawn to the cross. Though the substitutionary death of Christ on the cross is of everlasting importance, and I do not want to lessen it for one moment, it is his humanity that is also to be seen as substitutionary. From the moment of his conception he took on to himself humanity *for us* and for our salvation, and at that moment began his ministry of redemption for all who call upon his name. More on this in the closing chapter.

10. See Matthew 1:18–20.

11. "The movement of God to man and man to God" is a phrase often used by Thomas F. Torrance.

12. "Saved" not only entails going to heaven but in the present living a holy life in and through and with Jesus in communion with the Holy Spirit to the glory of the Father.

truly deny Jesus is fully human. Note that with "became flesh," we are to understand that his humanity "became" (see the first note for John 1:14). It is important to confess that his humanity is *not* eternal. If it were, then his life from conception to ascension would not represent us because he would not be human as we are. As we see in Hebrews 2:14–17, if Jesus is not human as we are (yet, of course, without sin [Heb 4:15]), he could not be our high priest and make atonement for us. So, his humanity, like ours, "became."

John teaches us that with Jesus we not only have a man, but also God among us. The phrases "dwelt among us," "we saw his glory," and "full of grace and truth" are filled with Old Testament themes that apply only to Yahweh. See the notes for these phrases. John holds, and so should we, that Jesus is Yahweh the Son.

One last thing concerning Jesus's humanity, and what we are in light of that. Ever wonder what is behind Matthew's mention of Jesus's temptation in the wilderness (Matt 4:1–11)? Here there are two parallels worth mentioning.

First, Jesus is "led up by the Spirit into the wilderness to be tempted by the devil." Then we read that Jesus fasted for "forty days and forty nights." Israel was in the wilderness for forty years, where its faith was tested and tried. And in that time Israel continually was brought under the judgment of the LORD for its disobedience. It is no coincidence that Matthew recalls the historic event of Jesus in the wilderness for forty days. I'll get right to the point: Jesus is the embodiment of Israel; he is Israel; he is the *new* Israel. What Israel failed to do, he did. And for his glory he did it *for* us so that by being included in him (John 17:21; 2 Cor 5:17) by grace through faith, we become Israel—the people of the triune God; we become the church!

Second, there is a parallel with the first man Adam. Adam was tempted and failed; Jesus was tempted and overcame. This is, in part, why Jesus is called by Paul "the last Adam" (1 Cor 15:45). Where Adam failed, Christ was triumphant *for* us (Rom 5:12–15). Thus, by grace through faith, not only are we brought into union with Jesus, we are also *in* Jesus. He with the Father and the Spirit has begun to make us a new creation (2 Cor 5:17), conforming us into what the first Adam was created to be. This is being conformed to the "image" (sound familiar!) of the Son of God the Father (cf. Rom 8:29), which begins through the indwelling of God the Holy Spirit.

So Jesus's humanity is true humanity, true humanity for reasons profound and glorious *for* us.

## What Jesus Says and Does, Yahweh Says and Does

This is one of many excellent ways to read the New Testament in the light of the Old Testament. From the Lord Jesus we have actions and words that can only be attributed to Yahweh as he is revealed in the Old Testament.

In addition to the Old Testament Scriptures speaking of Yahweh that have been applied to Jesus in John 1:14 (see the chart above), let's look at two more.

First is Matthew 8:23–27 and the stilling of the storm. Take a moment to read Matthew 8:23–27. Now take a moment to read Psalm 107:23–29. Notice any parallels between the two passages? There are direct correspondences: boats on the sea; witnessing the great works of the LORD; being terrified; crying out to the LORD; and the LORD stilling the storm. The main point of Matthew is to illustrate in what way we have Immanuel—God *with* us (Matt 1:23).[13] Jesus himself is the divine presence[14] of God—God with his people. He is the LORD of Psalm 107!

The second example is Matthew 24:30–31, and like Matthew 8, it falls within this Gospel's two bookends (God with us [1:23; 28:20]). Our focus is on the theme of "cloud rider." Jesus claims he is going to come "on the clouds of the sky" (Matt 24:30). In Isaiah 19:1 "the LORD is riding on a swift cloud." The context of these

13. The Gospel of Matthew furnishes for us two bookends for "God with us." There is of course Matthew 1:23, but the closing bookend is Matthew 28:20, where Jesus states, "I am with you always." In between these two bookends is content to explain how Jesus was "with us." See the next example below.

14. This also applies to the Holy Spirit. See the "Basics" section of the next chapter.

two passages will grab you. In Matthew the context is judgment (24:29–31), just like it is in Isaiah. And see also Daniel 7:13–15. There, "one like a son of man" coming on the clouds is given dominion, glory, and a kingdom that will be everlasting; and all people in his kingdom will serve him.

## The Creed of Chalcedon, Hebrews 2:14–17, and the Twofold Movement

Above we read a brief word on a particular portion of the Chalcedonian Creed. For the sake of quick reference I reproduce it here:

> Jesus possesses two natures, divine and human, in union one with the other. Each nature is possessed in its fullness. The two natures are *united*, not mixed and not divided. Jesus is *homo-ousios* with the Father according to the Godhead, and *homo-ousios* with us according to the Manhood.

When we speak of the relation of the two natures of Jesus—deity and humanity—the word we should use is "union." The two natures of Christ are "unioned," not mixed into one another nor separated one from the other. Let's look at some negative implications if the two natures are mixed and if they are separated.

If they are mixed, is Jesus *truly* a human as we are? No. He becomes a hybrid human, human mixed with the divine. To mix the two natures of Jesus into a single hybrid nature leads to the heresies of Monophysitism and Eutychianism. With this type of Christology Jesus is not like us in every way (Heb 2:14, 17). In this passage in Hebrews, there are purposes for Jesus being like us in every respect (though again, without sin): to render the devil powerless; to free believers from being enslaved to the fear of death; to be our faithful and merciful high priest; and to make atonement. The full humanity of Jesus must be confessed and held as a posture of worship on our parts if accurate and precise worship is to take place.

What if we jettison the biblical teaching of the union of the two natures and instead separate the two natures, as did Nestorianism? Doing so can lead to the view that there are two separate persons, which results merely in an external, moral relation between deity and humanity. This is to say, there would be no intimate and close *union* of God and humanity in the person of Jesus, but rather a distant separation of deity and humanity that can only be brought together by a mere morally human Jesus. Thus, there would be no movement of the triune God to humanity and of humanity to the triune God in the one person of Christ. To separate is to sever, and thus a Nestorian Jesus cannot as both God and man as one person experience thirst, crying, and dying. Jesus as God could never, in the view of Nestorianism, experience what we experience; only his humanity experienced what we experience, thus threatening the solidarity between us and God the Son brought on by the union of the two natures. To reiterate, with the one person of Jesus who is both God and man, we have precisely to do with the reconciliation of the triune God to us, and of us to the triune God.

So regarding Jesus's two natures, interesting questions arise, the answers to which can be false or true. Here's the issue: What now do we do about the words and acts of Jesus (and let's not forget—in unbreakable union with the Father and the Spirit)? What should we think when we read of Jesus saying "I am"? What should we think about Jesus dying?

First, here are some troubling answers in light of the discussion above. As we saw, if we hold to the view that Jesus's two natures are mixed (as in Monophysitism or Eutychianism), then Jesus's life is not vicarious or substitutionary *for us humans*. As a result, his thirsting, his weeping, his death on a cross, and his resurrection and ascension were not accomplished for us. If Jesus was not truly human but a hybrid "human," we would not be resurrected with him in all his identity as man. If he was not true humanity, then he could not be our high priest and make atonement for us. We would never be reconciled to God the Father (Rom 5:10–11).[15]

---

15. Reconciled *to* the Father, *through* Christ, *in* the Holy Spirit. Reconciliation, like other doctrines, takes place in the life of the Holy Trinity.

What if we separate the two natures of Christ into two persons (as in Nestorianism)? Consider when Jesus said "I am." As mentioned above, if there is separation, then Jesus as one person did not say "I am"; only his divine nature or person said that. Thus he as one person did not say "I am" and therefore could not *himself* as both God and man be the movement of God to us and for us, and us to God. Further, if there is a separation of the divine and human, what of Jesus's death on the cross? Jesus himself as one person was not the atoning sacrifice. The one incarnate God the Son did not die for us.

But Jesus, God the Son, *did* die for us. If we look at the Creed of Chalcedon we read that Jesus possesses, in union, two natures as "one person." This is strongly implied throughout the New Testament, is it not? "*Jesus* said," not "the God part of Jesus said"; "*Jesus* wept," not "the human part of Jesus wept." And "*Jesus* died," not "the human part of Jesus died."

Mystery of mysteries! Let us worship this Christ to the glory of God the Father and in communion with God the Holy Spirit.

## Discussion

1. Look that the prologue to the Gospel of John (1:1–18), pick one or two themes (suggestion: one not already covered in this chapter) in the prologue, and locate a verse or a passage beyond the prologue to see how they are "fleshed out."

2. Why is it important that Jesus is *homo-ousios* with the Father according to his deity, and *homo-ousios* with us according to his humanity?

CHAPTER 4

# God the Holy Spirit

W e now enter into Pneumatology. We should be mindful that pneumatology is not to be severed from Patrology and Christology. The Holy Spirit is always God the Holy Spirit in eternal relation with God the Father and God the Son. The Trinity of Father, Son, and Holy Spirit is a Trinity of being in a relationship of *homo-ousios* and *peri-choresis*.

## The Basics

The designation "Holy Spirit," though biblical, can communicate to the unaware that the Holy Spirit is some kind of impersonal entity. For example, Jehovah's Witnesses think that "holy spirit"[1] is "Jehovah's active force."[2] What must be understood from the outset is that the Holy Spirit is both God and a person.

## The Holy Spirit Is God

We confess that the Holy Spirit is "God the Holy Spirit," the third person of the Trinity. Why?

1. Notice the lack of "the" and the intently lower-case for "holy" and "spirit."

2. Their translation of Genesis 1:2: "and God's active force was moving about over the surface of the waters." https://www.jw.org/en/library/bible/study-bible/books/genesis/1/.

Paul, being in his words "a Hebrew of Hebrews; as to the Law, a Pharisee" (Phil 3:5), knew of the biblical teaching of the "divine presence"—God dwells with his people. Paul in the strongest of terms understands that the Holy Spirit is God who dwells with and in the people of the triune God. In 1 Corinthians 3:16 and 6:19, Paul instructs Christians with these words: "Do you not know that you[3] are a temple of God and *that* the Spirit of God dwells in you?" and "Or do you not know that your[4] body is a temple of the Holy Spirit within you?" This recalls Paul's "body of Christ" teaching in 1 Corinthians 12. The body of Christ is the temple of the Holy Spirit.

In the Old Testament, one theological truth stands out starkly: the divine presence of Yahweh with his people. In Isaiah 43:2, the LORD says, "When you pass through the waters, I will be with you." Genesis 26:24: "The LORD appeared to him the same night and said, 'I am the God of your father Abraham; Do not fear, for I am with you.'" Genesis 28:15: "Behold, I am with you and will keep you wherever you go." Further, in both the tabernacle and the temple of Israel was the presence of the LORD (Exod 40:34–35; Ezek 10:4).

It is not mere coincidence that Paul equates the reality of the divine presence of the LORD with the presence of God the Holy Spirit in the temple, which is the body of Christ. Paul sees the Holy Spirit as God, in no uncertain terms. It is interesting that, as the New Testament unfolds, Christ's physical body is the temple (John 1:14; 2:19) in which the glory of the Lord dwells, and then the body of believers becomes the temple in which the glory of the Lord Holy Spirit dwells (1 Cor 3:19; 6:19).

## The Holy Spirit Is a Person

Several attributes of personhood are recorded in the New Testament that testify to God the Holy Spirit as a person.

3. Plural "you."
4. Plural "your."

First, Jesus uses "him" and "he" when referring to the Holy Spirit[5] (John 16:7-8, 13).[6] In John 14:16-17, Jesus also alludes to the theme of divine presence when he tells us that the Spirit will be "with" the disciples as well as "in" them, and in that very passage tells the disciples that he is going to send to them "another helper."[7] Only a *person* can be called a helper in the sense of the Holy Spirit's role in the world and the church. He convicts the world of sin, righteousness, and judgment (John 16:8); guides into all truth; hears, speaks, discloses, and glorifies Jesus (John 16:13-15). Only a person is capable of doing these things.

Additionally, God the Holy Spirit can be grieved (Eph 4:30). The Holy Spirit speaks, answers prayer, sets apart workers and calls them, sends out workers, and refers to himself with the personal pronoun "me" (Acts 13:2-4).

5. There is much more involved in concluding that the Holy Spirit is a person than Jesus using "he" and "him," as we will see above. We need to keep in mind that both the Father and the Holy Spirit do not possess gender as we know it. The Father and the Spirit are genderless. But we must also keep in mind that (1) Jesus employs "he" and "him"; and (2) the Father reveals himself as Father. Some may call attention to the fact that the masculine pronouns "he" and "him" are used precisely because in John 16:7-8 the noun for "helper" or "comforter" is masculine (*paracletos*). In Greek, pronouns must match the gender of the noun to which they refer; so John, as he records Jesus's statement, had to use the masculine pronouns "he" and "him" to refer to the masculine noun for "comforter." However, in John 16:13 the noun for "Spirit" (*pneuma*) is neuter in the phrase "the Spirit of truth," referring to the Holy Spirit. The first part of verse 13 reads, "But when he, the Spirit of truth, comes." John, it seems, breaks a rule of Greek grammar by using a masculine pronoun for a neuter noun.

6. I often ask Jehovah's Witnesses whether or not they will refer to the Holy Spirit in the same way that Jesus referred to the Holy Spirit. They believe that "holy spirit" is the impersonal force of Jehovah and use the pronoun "it." I ask them to read, in their translation, John 16:7-8, 13.

7. Or "comforter, advocate."

## Discussion

1. Read 1 Corinthians 12 (on the church as the body of Christ) and look for trinitarian theology. In other words look for the unified divine activity of the Father and the Son and the Holy Spirit.

2. Think about Jesus referring to the Holy Spirit as "another helper." Besides "helper" being a term implying personhood, what does "another" imply?

## Beyond the Basics

God the Holy Spirit is Deity. In Christian theology, deity implies divine personhood, so deity and personhood must be inextricably linked. As a result of the testimony of the Old and New Testaments, the theologians of the Nicene-Constantinopolitan Creed confessed the Holy Spirit as "the Lord, the giver of life, who proceeds from the Father. With the Father and the Son he is worshiped and glorified." These are strong words of worshipful adoration! Let's explore a few of these phrases.

## The Lord

To confess the Holy Spirit as Lord is to acknowledge his sovereign rule over all things, including the church, which is the body of Christ and the temple in which he dwells. As the divine presence in the church, the Holy Spirit goes before us, just as Yahweh did with ancient Israel as he dwelled in the tabernacle and temple. Think of the worshipful respect and longing for holiness that came from the believers of Israel because of that reality, and let us think in the same way when it comes to the indwelling divine presence of the Holy Spirit.

## The Giver of Life

Another amazing title. Recall Genesis 1:2: "the Spirit of God was moving over the surface of the waters." This is a creative act on the part of the Holy Spirit, and the early theologians no doubt had Genesis in mind when they issued the creed. Also, to call the Holy Spirit "the giver of life" is to place him precisely in equality with Jesus, of whom John states, "In him was life" (John 1:4). John here is telling us that Jesus created all things (an allusion to Genesis 1 [remember the first three words of the Gospel of John?]), and as creator (with the Father and the Spirit) he is able to give eternal life (John 3:16). Through indwelling, the Holy Spirit is the giver of eternal life. But remember, it is not as if Jesus gives life and then the Holy Spirit gives life, as if to say they give life in separation from each other. Rather, due to the Father and the Son and the Holy Spirit being eternally *homo-ousios* with *peri-choresis*, the three persons together, simultaneously in inseparable harmony, give life.

## With the Father and the Son
## He Is Worshiped and Glorified

When we worship the Holy Spirit, we at the same time worship the Father and the Son, and worship the Father and the Son and the Holy Spirit as one God. As regards the distinction of persons, worship of each distinct divine person is appropriate. And as we worship each distinct person, we must immediately be drawn to the oneness of the Holy Trinity. In other words, as soon as we find ourselves worshiping a distinct person of the Trinity, we also find ourselves mindful of the one God.

Though the Nicene-Constantinopolitan Creed does not specifically state that the Holy Spirit is *homo-ousios* with the Father and the Son, to confess the Holy Spirit as Lord and the giver of life, and to worship him, leaves no room to deny that the Holy Spirit is *homo-ousios* with the Father and the Son. As a result, we pray to the Holy Spirit just as we pray to the Father and the Son. And due to *homo-ousios*, to pray to the Holy Spirit is to honor simultaneously the Father and the Son! To give glory to God the Holy Spirit is to give *at the same time* glory to the Father and the Son. Those who honor the Holy Spirit honor the Father and the Son.

Finally, let's do some interpretive, Trinity-related exercises together by considering some of the Scripture verses and passages brought up in the "Basics" section on the Holy Spirit.

The first exercise involves 1 Corinthians 3:16 and 6:19: "Do you not know that you are a temple of God and *that* the Spirit of God dwells in you?" and "Or do you not know that your body is a temple of the Holy Spirit within you?" With these two Scriptures taken together, we shall now look for three themes.

First, in the first Scripture (3:16), what is the predicate for "God"? To answer that question we move to the beginning of 1 Corinthians, specifically 1:3: "God our Father." So the predicate for "God" in 3:16 is the Father. Also, the Holy Spirit is called "the Spirit of God [the Father]." Moreover, look at the connection between "temple of God [the Father]" and "the Holy Spirit of God [the Father] dwells in you." There is a relationship between the Father and the Spirit that we can see when we are aware of *homo-ousios* between the Father and the Spirit: We are the temple belonging to God the Father *and* to God the Holy Spirit who indwells that temple!

Second, and we looked at this earlier, in both verses the Holy Spirit is the divine presence in the temple, which is the body of Christ.

Third, compare "temple of God [the Father]" in 3:16 with "temple of the Holy Spirit" in 6:19. Paul equates the temple of God the Father with the temple of the Holy Spirit. Due to *homo-ousios* and *peri-choresis* the connection is so much more understandable!

Look with me at another passage where knowledge of *homo-ousios* and *peri-choresis* leads to deep Christian thinking. In John 14:16, Jesus says, "I will ask the Father, and he will give you another Helper, that he may be with you forever." It is plain enough to see that the three persons are here listed, but there are several things that theologically lie beneath the surface.

First, Jesus as the obedient Son of the Father defers to the Father by asking him to give to the disciples another Helper, the Holy Spirit. The three persons act in unity in *homo-ousios* and *peri-choresis* relation.

Second, how can Jesus be sure the Father will answer "yes" to his request? Jesus as fully man and fully God the Son is one (*homo-ousios*) with the Father and is perfect humanity (*homo-ousios* with us according to the humanity) for our sake. Therefore, Jesus as both God and man knows the Father's will, and part of the reason he knows the Father's will is because as a man he is indwelled by God the Holy Spirit! His request is made perfect and complete in himself but also in the Father and in communion with the Spirit.

Finally, the Helper that Jesus requests of the Father, the Helper that is *homo-ousios* with Jesus and the Father, is the very Holy Spirit that dwells in us (as his temple), just as he dwells in the man Christ Jesus forever.

It is important to confess the Holy Spirit as God the Holy Spirit because only a divine person can do all the things we learned about above. We thus should adoringly worship him to the glory of the Father and the Son, for by worshiping him, we worship the Father and the Son and acknowledge the oneness of the Father and the Son and the Holy Spirit.

## Discussion

1. Read Ephesians 2:18. We certainly see trinitarian theology there! Think about the role of the Holy Spirit in this verse. See if you can theologize pneumatologically (see Pneumatology) about who the Holy Spirit is and what he does.

2. We saw that with God the Holy Spirit we have the divine presence in the temple (the body of Christ). Employing *homo-ousios* and *peri-choresis*, how is the presence of the Holy Spirit in us at the same time the presence of Jesus and the Father in us?

# CHAPTER 5

## *Bringing It Together*

A short book like this cannot cover every Christian doctrine, so it must be selective. In this chapter we look again at important issues and some select doctrines. The order in which these occur is not meant to convey a logical or systematic order. As mentioned throughout this book, all doctrines and all they communicate should be seen within the life of the triune God. This is the business of theology, which of course includes our worship.

### An Ambiguous "God"?

"God *is* the Trinity, and the Trinity *is* God."[1] The triune God is the only God that truly is, but do we really think that way and worship with that in mind and heart?

We often speak of "God" in ways that sound so generic that it is difficult to tell the difference between Christians and "religious" non-Christians. When many people (Christians *and* non-Christians) speak of "God," overwhelmingly we hear talk of a generic God and thus a replacement of "God" for the Holy Trinity. What about TV news shows? Are there any predicates heard for "God"? When professional athletes thank God after a game, I wonder all the time just who it is they are thanking and whether or not *they* know who it is they are thanking. And when people we

1. Torrance, *Trinitarian Faith*, 330.

know are Christians take the public platform to speak and all we hear is "God," should we not wonder what non-Christians in the audience think when they hear that word? And what about our corporate worship as the body of Christ? Is it accurate and precise when mentioning "God"?

As stated earlier, "God" can be an empty slogan. Even the phrase "almighty God" is ambiguous. In fact, it is non-creedal, for the Council of Nicaea was careful to state "God the Father Almighty." This phrase strongly communicates that it is through, and in the light of, the Son that God is called Father.

How much is all the above important for the holy life and worship of the church? For accurate and precise worship (in all its forms, including music, prayer, preaching and teaching, etc.), clarity is needed to aid and therefore enrich the worship experience as both mind and heart are joined, they being two sides of the same coin. It is the right thing to do, lest we trivialize God. The Holy Trinity must be worshiped and adored as we live in holiness in ways that are fitting to and correspond with his revelation to us in Jesus Christ.

## One Personal Being, Three Persons

What should we say about how "three" relates to "one"?[2] As we saw in Chapter 1, the three persons are the one God and the one God is three persons. But is the one God actually personal? If so, how so? And is this even important? These are tremendously important questions. Because we, *as persons*, worship, and worship includes personal relationship with the object of our worship. For proper personal relation in worship, we must be mindful that we are worshiping a personal triune God.

Two doctrines place us squarely in the right place to answer the question of whether or not we worship an ambiguous God or a personal triune God. In light of *peri-choresis*, the mutual

---

2. When I ask Christians to describe the doctrine of the Trinity in a short phrase, I usually hear, "Three in One." But we must ask ourselves, "Three *what* in One *what*?"

indwelling of the three distinct persons, the one God is therefore personal and should be addressed in the singular and in a personal way. In light of *homo-ousios*, the three distinct persons share the same being. Put another way, if the three persons mutually indwell each other (while remaining distinct) *as persons*, and if the three persons share the same being or God-ness, then we should conclude that the one God is the personal divine triune being. Thus, "one personal being/God as three persons" or "three persons as one personal being/God."

But now the sticky issue of the pronoun for God. What pronoun do we employ when addressing the one God? The center, the *controlling* center, that provides the answer is the man Jesus Christ. Jesus as both God and man is the second person of the Trinity. In the light of Jesus being a man, and in light of the Trinity being God and God being Trinity, do we want to employ "it" for God? Do we want to employ "she"? Take a few moments thinking about where you want to land on these questions.[3]

## How to Do Theology and Worship

We often presuppose, whether knowingly or under the surface, that doctrines are "separate" doctrines. Of course we have to talk of them in their respective categories, but all the while we should realize that they exist within the life of the Holy Trinity. In short, it is wrong to sever or partition doctrines from the mooring in which they are found—the triune God. The same goes for the doctrine and practice of worship.

The reason for this is twofold. First, the triune God is eternal, and therefore before creation nothing "was" but the Holy Trinity. Second, doctrines "became" because the triune God reveals

---

3. When people answer the pronoun question, there is often an unstated assumption that first there is "God" and then (if it ever comes up at all) there is Trinity. They proceed with an abstract notion of "God" in separation from the Holy Trinity and the Holy Trinity's self-naming as Father, Son, and Holy Spirit. This erroneous assumption carries through to the conclusion that "God" can be called "Mother" or referred to as "It."

himself to his creatures who "became," and in that revelation of himself we have the actual acts and words of the triune God in Christ, which become acts and words articulated verbally by his creatures.

We should realize that because all doctrines are inseparably linked to the Trinity, all doctrines themselves are linked inseparably. For examples, salvation is tied to resurrection; the virgin birth is tied to salvation and resurrection; reconciliation is tied to salvation and the resurrection and the virgin birth. In short, all doctrines are inseparable from the Trinity and are inseparable from one another.

Let's look at a number of Christian doctrines and view them within the life of the Trinity.

## In the Beginning

We know the triune God because the triune God first revealed himself to humanity. For his own good and perfect and loving desire to commune actively through his presence with humanity, humanity was meant to enjoy the presence of God intimately in the revealing of himself *for* humanity. In doing so, the Holy Trinity made a special covenant with Adam and Eve, desiring an intimate relationship with them and the rest of his good creation. In Genesis 2 this relationship with the LORD (Yahweh) involved the vertical and horizontal—simultaneously a relationship with the triune God and with one another. All was good.

But then sin entered into the relationship and the pure good became corrupt (Gen 3). Sin had broken the perfect and good relationship between the holy one and humanity. Things were fallen on our part, and we began to see ourselves as the center of the universe. Worship of the Holy Trinity of God was replaced by worship of ourselves. Adam and Eve were banished from his direct presence in the Garden of Eden. So began the rest of the long, long history of humanity, steeped in rebellion. Though there were those who were faithful, still there were those who remained in autonomous rebellion.

From the beginning it was meant that Adam and Eve and all their offspring would enjoy the fruit of being justified and sanctified (see soteriology, justification, and sanctification). We all were meant to live a life of intimate relationship with the LORD and with each other, in worship of the only one who is worthy of worship.

So where was the LORD in all this?

The LORD was not finished yet!

## After the Beginning

Out of self-giving love the triune God offered forgiveness to the very humanity that pushed him away in self-avowed exaltation of itself. The LORD intended to bring humanity back to the relationship established in Genesis 2.

In spite of the envy and strife and self-exaltation and murder and a host of other vices that plagued humanity, the LORD was gracious. Yahweh, so that humanity would know him, reached to and for a lost humanity and began to make a series of covenants with and through certain chosen servants: Adam (Gen 2), Noah (Gen 9), Abraham (Gen 12; 15; 17), Moses (Exod 24), and David (2 Sam 7). In those times, the Father, through the active presence of his Son or Word (the Logos of John 1:1) and in the Holy Spirit, would not allow humanity to fall headlong into the abyss of sin and death. Through all this, even in Old Testament times, anyone who called upon the name of the LORD enjoyed the beginning of being conformed to the original image of Adam.

## The Coming of Jesus

In the fullness of time, God the Father sent his Son to be born of the virgin Mary (Gal 4:4). At the moment of the incarnation of the Logos of the Father (John 1:1) by the agency of the Holy Spirit (Matt 1:18, 20), the real presence of Yahweh with his people as recorded in the Old Testament was pushed to the profoundest level—God himself dwelt among us (John 1:14) in the fullness of his Spirit (Luke 4:1) in the fullness of humanity. Filled with his Holy Spirit, the same Holy Spirit with whom Jesus eternally shared oneness of deity in *homo-ousios* and *peri-choresis* with the Father, Jesus in the power of the Holy Spirit began his reconciliation of humanity to the Father, living for us and for his glory a substitutionary perfect and sinless life (Heb 4:15), brought to the cross as the obedient servant of the Father (Acts 3:26) in fulfillment of the words of Isaiah (52:13—53:12).

This Jesus, who in the words of the Nicene Creed is true God from true God and *homo-ousios* with the Father, came for us and for our salvation as both God and man. And the apostle John knew this well. He records Jesus's words that Jesus is the way, and the truth, and the life, and that no one comes to the Father but through him (John 14:6). By means of Jesus (and the Holy Spirit) we know the Father. This is knowing in covenant. Salvation entails knowing the Father and the Son and the Holy Spirit, and knowing them all at once as Trinity. Knowing the triune God this way means that "we have the mind of Christ" (1 Cor 2:16). We cannot possess the mind of Christ apart from the life of the Holy Trinity, "for through him [Christ] we both have our access in one Spirit to the Father" (Eph 2:18).

## Knowing the Triune God

How do we know God as the Father and the Son and the Holy Spirit? Let's start with a brief confession: The Father reveals himself *through* the Son and *in* the Holy Spirit. Three observations now follow.

First, note that we must never isolate Patrology from Christology from Pneumatology, because the three distinct persons of the Trinity are inseparable, which of course is pointed to by *homo-ousios* and *peri-choresis*.

Second, note the prepositions in the confession. Stated there are "through" and "in." "Through" means "by means of"; "in" means "in communion with." Knowing the Father *by means of* the Son and *in communion with* the Holy Spirit implies that we know

God the Son and God the Holy Spirit in order to know God the Father through the Son and in the Spirit. One thing we conclude from this is that the Son reveals the Father (John 1:18) to us as he himself is indwelled by his Holy Spirit; and the Son reveals the Father to us at the very moment the Holy Spirit indwells us.

Third, implied in the phrase "knowing the triune God" is relationship. There should be an act of the mind and heart in faith in knowing the three persons, and worship must follow accordingly in that knowledge.

## A Blessing from Jesus: We Enter into the Knowing between the Father and the Son

Earlier we looked at Luke 10:22, where we read Jesus saying that no one knows who the Son is except the Father, and no one knows who the Father is except the Son, and those to whom the Son chooses to reveal the Father. The miraculous entering of us into the unique knowing between the Father and the Son takes place through the Son at the very moment we enter into relationship with the Son in communion with the Holy Spirit. This is, to use a phrase from Paul, to "have the mind of Christ" (1 Cor 2:16).

Athanasius delivered to us a short essay on this very verse. Interesting, but not surprising, is that this essay is filled with quotations from the Gospel of John! In this work, he stressed continuously that the Son is "proper" to the Father. Though Athanasius did not specifically use the word *homo-ousios*, this is what he meant by "proper." Athanasius meant that Jesus, the Son of God incarnate, is all that the Father is, except Father. What might we learn from him through his short treatise?[4]

First, the Father knowing the Son and the Son knowing the Father occur within the *homo-ousios* relationship between Father and Son, and thus within the life of the triune God. As only God can reveal God, so also only God can know God as Father and Son.

4. For the following I am indebted to Torrance, *Trinitarian Faith*, 302–13; Torrance, *Theology*, 215. These points appear in Tsoukalas, "Do Christians and Muslims," 324–25.

Second, the incarnation of the Son occurs within the life of the triune God. With the doctrine of the virgin conception and birth of Jesus we see the Father sending the Son to incarnate in the womb of Mary by the agency of the Holy Spirit (Matt 1:18, 20). This is an example of how doctrines cannot be severed from the life of the Trinity. Thus, we must not separate the doctrine of the incarnation from the doctrine of the Trinity, for in Luke 10:22 it is the incarnate Son who speaks these words.

Third, there is a mutual, intimate knowing between the Father and the Son. Only the Father and the Son (and the Holy Spirit [1 Cor 2:11]) know each other in the fullest sense.

Fourth, note "and anyone to whom the Son wills to reveal *him* [the Father]." On our parts, by the grace of the triune God revealed in Jesus, and thus by grace through faith in Jesus, we enter into the mutual knowing between the Father and the Son, albeit finitely. Because only the Father and the Son and the Holy Spirit know each other in the fullest sense in their trinitarian relations, only they in their relations of *homo-ousios* and *peri-choresis* know each other exhaustively. But amazingly, we are brought into their mutual knowing to the measure they allow!

Fifth, strongly implied in this verse is that on our parts, knowledge of the Son and knowledge of the Father arise together. To know the Son is, at the same time, to know the Father (and the Spirit). Put another way, knowing the Father comes with, and is the simultaneous result of, knowing the Son. Think of how often we have assumed, non-critically, that first we know Jesus and then after that we know the Father. Have we often operated under that assumption?[5]

So what of all this? One thing stands out: If we know whom we worship, then we should worship whom we know. Moreover, when we worship, we worship standing within and sharing in the mutual knowing between the Father and the Son. Our worship actually occurs within this relationship!

---

5. Once rid of this assumption, will this affect what we say when we witness to others?

## Jesus Our Great High Priest and Mediator

We worship *with* Jesus as our great high priest and mediator, in communion with God the Holy Spirit, who as well is given to us for our salvation. Indeed, worship is set squarely in the life of the triune God—worship of the triune God *with* Jesus in the reality of the vertical and the horizontal made perfect by his presence.

Our salvation has as its foundation the miraculous doctrine of Jesus as our "great high priest" (Heb 4:14). We are also told in Hebrews 2:17 that Jesus is the "faithful high priest," and in 1 Timothy 2:5 the "one mediator." With God the Son—Jesus of Nazareth, the Logos of the Father—we have the miraculous event that occurred simultaneously at the moment of the conception and subsequent birth of Jesus: The incarnate Jesus is (1) the movement of the triune God to humanity, and (2) the movement of humanity to the triune God. How? Why?

Perhaps the most astounding and inconceivable event in the history of the universe is that God the Son came to his creation as one of us (this answers "how?"), as one of his own creations! At his conception in the womb of Mary, Jesus took on a vicarious and full humanity *for* us (this answers "why?"). Thus, having been sent by God the Father to incarnate in the womb of the virgin Mary by the agency of God the Holy Spirit, God the Son as man began at the conception his substitutionary role for us. And he became for us and in our place the man indwelled by the Holy Spirit living a vicarious life pleasing to God the Father. Can you see the two-way movement? In this one miraculous event of the incarnation, the triune God sends himself to us in Jesus; and Jesus's very life is, in himself, the actual event of humanity's worshipful response to the Father in communion with the Holy Spirit. With this (among other things) the Holy Trinity is worthy of worship.

Why and how are we to worship? We should begin with the indicative—who Jesus is and who he is for us. In the Scriptures we see that Jesus is fully *theos* and fully human; two natures, each possessed in their fullness by the one person of Christ (see John 1:1, 14). In the very person of Jesus we have the perfect wedding of God and humanity; and thus with Jesus, by virtue of his being both God and man, we have the movement of God to us *by him* and us to God *by him*. The movement of God to us occurs in the historic reality of the incarnation, and of us to God in his vicarious and perfect humanity. Now comes the imperative: Worship! Worship, then, follows upon the fact of the incarnation and takes place within the sphere of the revealed Son of God in time and space.

In this two-way movement of great high priest and mediator, Jesus is in himself *for us*. Once again *homo-ousios* rises to the center! The two senses of *homo-ousios* mentioned in the Creed of Chalcedon are as follows: *homo-ousios* with the Father, according to deity; *homo-ousios* with us, according to his humanity. These two senses are vital to understanding Jesus as the movement of "for us and for our salvation."[6] The triune God comes to us in Jesus, and we come to the triune God in and with Jesus. Mindful worship of Jesus in this way is worship with precision!

## What Happened to "With"?

Unfortunately, the preposition "with" has largely been forgotten in Christian thought. Much is said of "in" and "through" Jesus (and rightly so), but "with" has become foreign to our worship.

A sad dynamic is alive here: we *state* that Jesus is with us (Matt 28:20), but we *worship* as if he is not. We must guard against the posture that the triune God stands above us across a great gulf and as a result becomes a "God up there" (see the Introduction, "The 'Great Gulf'") where our worship becomes something *performed to* the Lord. If we worship *with* Christ, our worship takes place simultaneously (due to *homo-ousios* and *peri-choresis*) in the real presence of God the Father and God the Holy Spirit; and in Christ and in communion with the Holy Spirit, our worship brings glory to the Father.

It is here, precisely, that the great truth of the high priesthood and mediatorship of the Lord Jesus crashes into this mindset of "a

6. This phrase is in both the Nicene-Constantinopolitan Creed and the Creed of Chalcedon.

God up there," into the mindset of "great gulfism." As a corrective to this malady, we confess that the incarnate Lord Jesus *in reality* is with us in the most profound[7] and dynamic of ways. And the Holy Spirit *in reality* is dynamically with us, indwelling us as the body of Christ in the reality of the ever-present Father.

How should this truth saturate the worship of the church? In the communion of the Holy Spirit, worship with Jesus takes place in the context of him as our great high priest and mediator. Thus Jesus takes our worship, sanctifies it (sets it apart and makes it holy), and presents it to the Father with us and for us. This truth applies to all forms of worship—music; preaching and teaching; taking communion; being baptized; praying. And here we must sound the alert and ask ourselves: Do we worship with the precision of the apostolic tradition revealed to us from the triune God in Jesus Christ? Is the music we sing godly, accurate, and precise? Is our preaching and teaching and witness the same? When we partake of the elements in communion, do we do so in worshipful acknowledgement that Jesus is with us *right now*, so much so that any concept or unconscious assumption of "great gulfism" is gone and forgotten? When we are baptized, or when we baptize someone, have we eliminated "performed down here to God up there" and replaced that with the real presence of Christ? When we pray "Our Father," are we aware that we are praying this *with* Jesus to the Father in real communion with the Holy Spirit?

Before reading on, take a moment to reflect on being mindful of the real presence of the triune God with us in Jesus Christ; and, by the grace and enabling of the Holy Spirit, meditate on that, thinking through what should characterize our worship.

---

7. Here we should be reminded that in Old Testament times, Yahweh was with his people. This is a historic truth to cherish. But the incarnation makes Yahweh's presence with his people a presence in the most profound and dynamic sense, for the Logos of God the Father, God the Son himself, became in the fullest sense one of us.

## The Church

Tied to the triune God, to knowing the triune God, to the incarnation, and to the great high priesthood and mediatorship of Christ is the church. We worship as the church, the body of Christ, the temple of God the Holy Spirit. We are now concerned with ecclesiology.

Look at Ephesians 2:19–21. We, the church, are "of God's household, having been built on the foundation of the apostles and prophets, Christ Jesus himself being the corner *stone*, in whom the whole building, being fitted together, is growing into a holy temple in the Lord, in whom you also are being built together into a dwelling of God in the Spirit."

It isn't difficult to see the Holy Trinity in this passage. "God" is God the Father (see Eph 1:2; predicates are important!). The church is the household (or, in Old Testament language, God the Father's family compound [see Chapter 2, "Beyond the Basics, God the Father as Patriarch"]). We have been built on the foundation (the tradition) of the prophets and the apostles, which is the rule or measure of the Christian faith. Christ is the corner stone, the first rock laid in building the temple, and the temple is the body of Christ. It is in him as the foundation that we are a holy temple (as "living stones" [1 Pet 2:5]), which is the dwelling of God the Holy Spirit (cf. 1 Cor 3:16; 6:19).

The church owes its existence, life, and calling to the triune God. The church therefore owes its existence and itself exists in the life of the Trinity, centered in the incarnation, life, death, resurrection, and ascension of Christ. In its existence in the life of the Holy Trinity, the church is one church, for in the Father and the Son and the Holy Spirit there is "one body and one Spirit . . . one Lord, one faith, one baptism, one God and Father of all who is over all and through all and in all" (Eph 4:4–6). Worship, then, should focus on the objective reality of the Father and the Son and the Holy Spirit in the union of their distinctive acts as the one God who is for us.

To reiterate, we have been built on the foundation or tradition of the prophets and the apostles. And since we are, it is absolutely required that our worship is GAWP, for it is the prophets and the apostles who, in communion with the Holy Spirit, have given to us the uniquely true and undefiled message and teachings of the triune God in history. The church exists in the very life of the Holy Trinity and as such is called in worship both to affirm and carry on "the rule of our faith,"[8] "the faith that was once for all handed down to the saints" (Jude 3). Worship, then, must be godly, accurate, and precise; and zeal for sound worship in sound doctrine is a must if the church is to continue as the church of Jesus Christ. Without sound doctrine and sound worship, the church will cease to be the church as defined in the Scriptures and in the apostolic tradition.

We are members of the Father's household because we have received Christ, having believed in his name (John 1:12); and in communion with God the Holy Spirit we live in union with the Father. In turn, the church is called to proclaim to a world without Christ the message of the gospel: "that Christ died for our sins according to the Scriptures, and that he was buried, and that he was raised on the third day according to the Scriptures" (1 Cor 15:3–4). We are commanded by the Lord of Glory himself to be baptized in the name of the triune God, to live in his name, and to make disciples (Matt 28:19) so that they too may live in the life of the triune God.

## The Church and the Triune God's Commands

Since the church owes its existence to the triune God, we are to act as members of the household of the Father (see above). There is much to say about *how* we are to live—the how and the what of it all. But *why?* is the first question.

*Why* is it that we are to obey God's commands? *Why* is it that we must "do"? Most of us have heard of the saying, "What would Jesus do?" Perhaps it should rather be this: "What *did* Jesus do?"

---

8. Irenaeus often employed this phrase and located the reality to which it pointed squarely in the foundation of the Father and the Son and the Holy Spirit. See Irenaeus, *Demonstration*, 38.

There is an amazing theological theme that permeates Scripture: "The indicative precedes the imperative." Though this phrase sounds somewhat intimidating, with a little explanation it is easy to grasp; and once you start looking for this theme, you will notice it consistently throughout the Bible.

"Indicative" refers to something done and/or who someone is. "I went to the market" is an indicative statement. So is "Carla is my boss." Imperative refers to a command: "Go to the market." If Carla my boss says to go to the market, I do so based on who she is. The indicative precedes the imperative.

For our purpose, the indicative refers to who the triune God is. It also refers to what the triune God has done (or is doing or will do). Imperatives or commands follow after that. So, commands to obey or to do something (including worship) always *follow* and are *based upon* who God is and what God has done. In short, because the triune God *did*, we are to *do*.

Here is an example from Scripture. It involves the command of the great commission[9] in Matthew 28. Jesus gives a command to make disciples of all nations (Matt 28:19). This is the imperative. But what are the indicatives that precede this imperative or command?

In verses 16 and 17 we see that Jesus appears on the mountain that he himself designates and calls (implied) the disciples to, and that the disciples worshiped him. To understand the utter divine depth of this act of Jesus, let's consider his words in the light of the Old Testament.

In the Old Testament, who appeared on a mountain to give commands? Yahweh did. Yahweh designated Sinai as the mountain where Moses would experience the divine presence, and called Moses to that mountain (Exod 19:18–20). Moses obeyed. Yahweh then gave to Moses the ten commandments (Exod 20) that Israel was to follow. But why did Moses, and why should Israel, obey the commands (imperatives)? Because of who Yahweh is and what he has done (indicatives). Just before the ten commandments

---

9. Or better, "CoMission," as Morton's book *Great CoMission* instructs. As we "go," Jesus is with us.

(imperatives) are given, they are preceded by an indicative: "I am the LORD your God, who brought you out of the land of Egypt" (Exod 20:2). Even prior to that occurs another indicative. In Exodus 3:14 Yahweh identified himself to Moses as "I AM." This is why Moses "did" and why Israel must "do." With this background we see that in Matthew 28:16–17 Jesus owns the divine right of both designating the mountain and appearing on it to give the command.[10] This explains why the disciples obeyed and worshiped Jesus.

Here is another indicative before we get to the command in verse 19. In verse 18 Jesus makes the claim that all authority has been given to him. He, as the Son of Man (see Dan 7:13–14), has all authority and his kingdom shall have no end.

Based upon all these indicatives, the command to make disciples follows (verse 19).

Matthew 28:16–20 occurs in the trinitarian context. Disciples of all the nations are to be baptized in the "name" (see AIRO) of the Trinity. It is not only the authority of Jesus with which we have to do, but also the authority of the Father and the Holy Spirit; not three separate "authorities" but one divine authority shared by the Father and the Son and the Holy Spirit (in *homo-ousial* and *perichoretic* relations).

## In Our Own Power?

In the section above, we learned that because the Holy Trinity *did* and *does*, we *do*—the indicative precedes the imperative. But *how* is it that we do?

As a preliminary to answering this question we revisit the diagnosis of Thomas F. Torrance mentioned in the Introduction. The doctrine of the Trinity has "tended to be lost from sight, and sometimes to be treated as rather irrelevant, or only of peripheral

10. Jesus is not only Yahweh the Son who appears on the mountain. He is also the new Moses as mediator who states the command to the people! In the one person of Christ we have God giving the command and mediating the command.

significance for Christian faith and living." For whatever reasons, it has been lost to many of us, resulting in devastating consequences for Christian life, including for holiness and worship.

"Devastating"? Isn't that just a little melodramatic?

When we hear the following answer to the question of *how* it is that we do, most of us are going to respond with, "Well, of course!" The answer to the question of *how* we do is this: by the grace of the indwelling and enabling ministry of God the Holy Spirit. Put another way, we do not live the Christian life under *our own* power, but with *the power of the Holy Spirit*.

But do we *really* think this way? How often have we sat through sermons or teaching where "We need to . . ." is void of mentioning the enabling grace of the Holy Spirit? Though "on paper" or theoretically many of us know that it is only by the enabling grace of the Holy Spirit that we do this or do that, why do we not state it clearly and often?

The sickness underlying this serious hole in our life and worship should by now come as no surprise. There is a profound lack of trinitarian theology in much of Christian thinking and speaking. If all aspects of worship (prayer, preaching and teaching, singing, theological conversation, living in holiness, etc.) occurred confessionally within the life of the Holy Trinity, this under-the-surface and subconsciously assumed mentality of self-empowering would be joyfully erased because trinitarian theology would *permeate* Christian articulation throughout. In short, if we by the gracious indwelling of God the Holy Spirit really become trinitarian in our understanding, the reality of the triune God would characterize our whole existence.

Behind this theology of self-empowering is "great gulfism." If there is a God at the other end of a vast gulf, then Christian understanding of life and worship becomes separated from God. As a consequence we place ourselves, at least unconsciously, externally apart from God and worship in a way that worship becomes "our worship" done toward God. But in reality, the Holy Trinity is *with us* by the real presence of Jesus in communion with the Holy Spirit, through whom we live in the Father's presence. We worship because the triune God does and did, and we "do" only by the empowering grace of the indwelling Holy Spirit, who with the Father and the Son lives in us and works in us to do good works in holiness. We are of the Father's "workmanship, created in Christ Jesus for good works, which God [the Father] prepared beforehand so that we would walk in them" (Eph 2:10).

"With Jesus, in the communion of the Holy Spirit and by the Spirit's grace and enabling, to the glory of the Father." This is not the only way to put it, but it is a way to put it. Whatever way we put it, it must be in a way that is trinitarian.

## The Worldwide Church Worships Simultaneously

Distinct gatherings of worshiping Christians are *not* autonomous—they are distinct within the whole. We often worship with the erroneous mindset (operating under the radar) that "our church is here and that church is there," as if we are worshiping in isolation from the rest of our brothers and sisters throughout the world. In reality, since the church as the *one* body of Christ worldwide owes its very existence to the everywhere-present triune God centered in the historic incarnation, life, death, and resurrection and ascension of Jesus, who is with us, we worship *with the whole church*. Therefore, though time zones be time zones, we worship as one church across the world. With Jesus and in communion with the Holy Spirit, we worship with the saints in South America with the saints in the United States of America with the saints in New Zealand with the saints in Canada with the saints in China because we as the one body of Christ worship with Christ.

## Points to Remember for Life and Worship

In this section I enumerate in very short fashion some points that we, by the enabling grace of God the Holy Spirit, should adopt for life and worship in the Father and the Son and the Holy Spirit.

1. The Holy Trinity is the foundation of all Christian doctrine.

2. Doctrine, which includes worshiping the triune God, centers around and in the person of God the Son, the Lord Jesus.

3. We worship *with* Christ our great high priest and mediator, who is "God with us."

4. The triune God—the Father and the Son and the Holy Spirit—is *really* with us; not just theoretically with us.

5. There is no great gulf between us and the triune God.

6. The empowering real presence of God the Holy Spirit, who indwells the church, is the "how?" of doing.

7. We do because Jesus does and did. We do because the Holy Trinity does and did.

8. We worship simultaneously with the whole church worldwide.

9. Use predicates in order to avoid speaking of a generic "God."

## Discussion

1. As God the Holy Spirit guides you right now, and in the real presence of the Holy Trinity, discuss key elements you will be mindful of in the worshipful act of Holy Communion.

2. Pray the prayer Jesus taught us to pray. As you pray with Jesus to the Father, practice being mindful of the indwelling presence of the Holy Spirit.

## A Prayer of Thanksgiving

Most gracious and Holy Trinity, our great God existing eternally as three persons, who was and is and evermore will be, thank you for your grace and mercy. Thank you, Father, for all things you provide through Jesus our Lord and Savior in communion with the Holy Spirit. Thank you, Jesus, for who you are and what you have done and do for us as our great high priest and mediator, to the glory of the Father and the Holy Spirit. Thank you, Holy Spirit, for indwelling the church, which as a gift from the Father is your temple and the body of Christ. We as the church throughout the world praise you, O Holy Trinity, as we will everlastingly, for you alone are worthy of worship and praise.

In the name of the Father and the Son and the Holy Spirit. Amen.

# Glossary

**AIRO** An acronym to help to remember the meanings of "name": authority; identity; reputation; ownership.

**Apollinarianism** Refers to the heresy (*see* Heresy) propagated by Apollinaris (fourth century). Apollinaris taught that the Logos (*see* Logos) replaced the human soul or mind of Jesus.

**Apostolic Tradition** The teaching of the apostles, in which and upon which the church stands, and which is the basis for the earliest creeds (*see* Creed; Nicene-Constantinopolitan Creed; Nicene Creed).

**Arianism** Propagated by Arius of Alexandria (*see* Arius). The heresy (*see* Heresy) setting forth that the Logos (*see* Logos) is a created being and not eternally God the Son.

**Arius** Arius of Alexandria (fourth century) was a notorious false teacher who denied that Jesus is of the same being (*see* Being) or nature (*see* Homo-ousios*) with the Father. *See* Arianism.

**Ascension** The enthronement of the resurrected Jesus to the "right hand of the Father." To occupy the place at the "right hand" refers in part to authority and rulership.

**Athanasius** Athanasius of Alexandria (fourth century) was one of the greatest theologians of the early church and a staunch defender of the doctrine (*see* Doctrine) of the Trinity.

**Atonement** The act of reconciling one party to another.

**Being, personal, of God** Being is "is-ness." (1) When considering the three persons, each distinct person of the Trinity is in
very being "very God." (2) When considering the tri-unity, the
triune (*see* Triune) God, the Holy Trinity, is also "very God."
The personal nature of the one triune being (God), the Holy
Trinity, comes from the relationship of the three distinct divine
persons in *homo-ousios* and *peri-choresis* (*see* Homo-ousios and
Peri-choresis).

**Chalcedon, Council of** An ecumenical council convened in AD
451 in order to settle the issue of how the two natures of Christ
relate to one another.

**Chalcedon, Creed of (Chalcedonian Creed)** The confession set
forth at the Council of Chalcedon in AD 451. *See* Chalcedon,
Council of.

**Christology** From the Greek words *christos* (Christ) and *logos*
(a word, discourse; *see* Logos). A discourse on the person of
Christ. Broadly refers to the study of Christ.

**Conception** In Christology (*see* Christology) this refers to the
moment when the eternal Son of God the Father, the Logos
(*see* Logos) sent by the Father, joined with himself a full human
nature in the womb of the virgin Mary by the agency of God
the Holy Spirit.

**Constantinople, Council of** An ecumenical council convened
in AD 381 to affirm the Nicene Creed (*see* Nicaea, Council of;
Nicene Creed; Nicene-Constantinopolitan Creed) and to add
to it more teaching pertaining to the Holy Spirit.

**Covenant** An agreement between two parties.

**Creed** From the Latin *credo* (I believe). A creed is a confession of
beliefs.

**Docetism** An early heresy (*see* Heresy) that challenged the church.
From the Greek *dokein* (to seem). Some forms of docetism pos-
ited that Jesus's body was illusory, while others stated that the
man Jesus was not truly human but made of heavenly flesh. In
either case, the true humanity of Jesus Christ was rejected.

**Deity** Either "God-ness" or a synonym for God.

**Doctrine** A teaching or a set of beliefs.

**Ecclesiology** From the Greek words *ecclesia* (church) and *logos* (a word; a discourse). *Ecclesia* comes from the Greek preposition *ek* (out of) and *kaleo* (I call); thus, "called-out ones." Broadly, ecclesiology refers to the study of the church.

**Eutychianism** Named after Eutyches (fourth to fifth centuries), who taught a form of monophysite (*see* Monophysitism) heresy (*see* Heresy). According to Eutyches, there was a moment when the union of the two natures took place, but at that moment the divine completely overwhelmed the human nature, and thus after this event Jesus possessed one nature, a nature that is not truly human.

**Faith** Trust. Faith is the posture of believing in someone or something. Faith does not occur "in a vacuum," so there is no such thing as "blind faith." Faith is an act of trusting based upon something(s) occurring before the act of faith. Faith can be grounded in something true or something false, so faith is not always right or true. Faith can also refer to a set of beliefs, as in the Christian faith.

***Filioque*** A Latin term meaning "and the Son." This phrase was later added to the Nicene-Constantinopolitan Creed (*see* Nicene-Constantinopolitan Creed), which reads, "the Holy Spirit . . . who proceeds from the Father." With the addition of *filioque* the confession reads, "the Holy Spirit . . . who proceeds from the Father *and the Son.*" Usually the year AD 1054 is given for the great schism between the Western tradition (at that time, the Roman Catholic Church) and the Eastern tradition (the Orthodox; *see* Western and Eastern Traditions), when the Western tradition adopted the *filioque* in its confession. The Eastern tradition, in order to distance itself further from the Western tradition (because much was at stake with the added clause), emphasizes "alone" with the Nicene-Constantinopolitan Creed: the Holy Spirit proceeds from the Father *alone.* Some theologians desire to see East and West come together on this doctrine of procession, and so have offered a middle way of understanding: the Holy Spirit proceeds from the Father *through* the Son. Early theologians like Cyril of Alexandria employed this way of phrasing it.

**GAWP** An acronym for "Godliness with Accuracy; Worship with Precision."

**Gnosticism** A very early heresy (*see* Heresy) that challenged the church. The word comes from the Greek *gnosis* (knowledge). Gnosticism comprises a wide variety of doctrines, all of which in their entirety cannot be said to characterize every gnostic sect. Yet, some general characteristics can be cited in a very loose sense: (1) a radical divide between the spiritual and the material or fleshly, where the spiritual alone, and to the disdain of the material, is the fount of truth; (2) the God of the Bible is not the high God, but a "demiurge," an egotistical "maker" claiming to be the high God but responsible for this scorned material creation; (3) the human soul is divine but trapped in a fleshly body; (4) the human soul eventually will return to the divine from which it came. In "Christian" expressions of Gnosticism, loosely held notions are (1) complete separation of the man Jesus from the heavenly "Christ"; (2) Jesus only appeared to be a man but was not (*see* Docetism); (3) Jesus only appeared to die on a cross and cannot be said to have resurrected bodily.

**Heresy** False teaching. That which is not in agreement with the Bible and therefore not in agreement with the early creeds that faithfully interpret the Scriptures.

***Homo-ousios*** Technically *homoousios*. From the Greek *homo* (one) and *ousios* (being, nature, essence). Thus "[of the] same being/ substance/nature/essence." This word was employed at the Council of Nicaea (AD 325; *see* Nicaea, Council of) to confess that Jesus is of the same being (*see* Being) or nature with the Father. Regarding the three persons of the Trinity, the Father and the Son and the Holy Spirit are eternally *homo-ousios*.

**Incarnate** *See* Incarnation.

**Incarnation** "In flesh." The act of the eternally pre-existent (*see* Pre-existence) Logos (*see* Logos) of the Father (John 1:1) becoming fully man (John 1:14).

**Irenaeus** One of the great theologians of the early church (second century). He is especially known for his *Against Heresies*, a voluminous treatise addressing the heresies (*see* Heresy) of Gnosticism (*see* Gnosticism).

**Justification** Being forgiven and accepted in Christ.

**Logos** The Greek word *logos* can mean simply "a word" or "a discourse," but in Christology (*see* Christology) it refers to "the Word," the eternally pre-existent (*see* Pre-existent) Son of God the Father.

**LORD** With small caps. In modern Old Testament translations "LORD" stands for the Hebrew YHWH (*see* Yahweh). YHWH is composed of four Hebrew consonants and is called the "tetragrammaton."

**Modalism** The heresy (*see* Heresy) that affirms only one person in the Godhead. In some expressions, the one person is the Father who becomes the Son who becomes the Holy Spirit. In other expressions the one person is Jesus who was the Father and became the Holy Spirit. Thus, one person; three modes (or manifestations).

**Monophysitism** The monophysite heresy (*see* Heresy) holds to a mixing of the two natures of Jesus into one nature, so that Jesus is not truly human as we are but is instead a hybrid composed of a mingling of the divine and human. This teaching was prevalent at the time of the Council of Chalcedon (*see* Chalcedon, Creed of).

**Monotheism** From the Greek *monos* (only, one), and *theos* (God; *see* Theos). The term refers to the belief-system asserting that one God, and one God only, exists or "is."

**Name** Employing the acronym AIRO, it refers to authority, identity, reputation, ownership.

**Nestorianism** Named after Nestorius (fourth to fifth centuries), though it is debated whether or not Nestorius himself actually held to the heresy (*see* Heresy) named after him. Nestorianism was popular during the time of the Council of Ephesus (AD 431) and the Council of Chalcedon (*see* Chalcedon, Creed of). Nestorianism places stress on the fact that the natures of Christ are independent and separated. As a consequence, ancient Nestorianism saw in Christ two persons rather than one. It promoted this view because of a refusal to say that Jesus as God thirsted or wept, or that Jesus as a man could say "I am."

**Nicaea, Council of** An ecumenical council convened in the city of Nicaea (now Iznik, Turkey) in AD 325, in large part to settle the issue of how Jesus relates to the Father.

**Nicene-Constantinopolitan Creed** A confession of beliefs asserted at the Council of Nicaea (*see* Nicaea, Council of; and Constantinople, Council of), with additional statements on the Holy Spirit. Often this creed is referred to simply as the Nicene Creed (*see* Nicene Creed). The Nicene-Constantinopolitan Creed was composed in AD 381.

**Nicene Creed** A confession of beliefs formulated in AD 325. Convened in large part to assert and settle the issue regarding how Jesus as God the Son relates to the Father. Against the Arian (*see* Arius; Arianism) heresy (*see* Heresy), it confessed that the Son is *homo-ousios* (of one being; *see* Being) with the Father. *See* Nicaea, Council of. *See* Nicene-Constantinopolitan Creed.

**Ontological** (*see* Ontologically).

**Ontologically** From the Greek word *ontos* (being). "Ontologically" (or "ontological") therefore refers to the "being-state" of someone; someone's nature or being. For example, "Ontologically I am human."

**Orthodoxy (orthodox)** Not to be confused with certain churches describing themselves as "Orthodox" (note upper-case "O"). (*See* Western and Eastern Traditions.) In the context of doctrine (*see* Doctrine) it is used as an adjective meaning teaching that gives right/correct honor to God; thus Christian "ortho-doxy" or "orthodox doctrine" (in both of these, note lower-case "o"). The word comes from the Greek *orthos* (correct, proper) and *doxa* (honor, glory).

**Patrology** A discourse on the person of God the Father. Broadly refers to the study of the Father. From the Greek *pater* (father) and *logos* (a word, discourse [*see* Logos]).

***Peri-chōresis*** Technically *perichōrēsis*. Co-inherence or mutual indwelling. The three persons of the Trinity mutually indwell each other in self-giving love. The distinctness of the persons, however, must at the same time be confessed.

**Person (persons)** A word pertaining individually to the Father and the Son and the Holy Spirit. We call the Father and the Son and the Holy Spirit "persons" in part because they relate to each other in dynamic, unified, and mutual self-giving love in eternal communion as Trinity.

**Predicate(s), theological** Words used theologically to define a subject. For "God," examples of proper predicates are God *the Father*; God *the Son*; God *the Holy Spirit*; the *triune* God.

**Pre-existent (Pre-existence)** When speaking of the Son, to "be" beforehand. In Christology (*see* Christology) it refers to the Word (the *logos*; *see* Logos) who eternally "is" "before" the event of the incarnation (see John 1:1, 14; *see* Incarnation).

**Pre-incarnate** Refers to the Logos (*see* Logos) of John 1:1 and to Jesus's eternal pre-existence (*see* Pre-existence) as God the Son.

**Pneumatology** A discourse on the Holy Spirit. Broadly refers to the study of the Holy Spirit. From the Greek words *pneuma* (spirit) and *logos* (a word, discourse [see Logos]).

**Presupposition** Something assumed beforehand.

**Reconciliation (Reconcile; Reconciling)** To be brought to fellow-ship in peace with another.

**Redemption** The act of obtaining something by paying a price and/or taking the place of others in order to free them. Christ's conception, birth, life, death, resurrection, and ascension all took place for us in order to redeem us and bring us to the place where reconciliation (*see* Reconciliation) between us and the Father takes place (see 2 Cor 5:18).

**Salvation** Includes many things. Salvation involves coming into a relationship with the triune God through Jesus Christ and obtaining all that Christ accomplished for us. As a result, salvation includes being saved from the eternal consequences of sin and living a life of holiness pleasing to God the Father in communion with the Holy Spirit.

**Sanctification** Being set apart to live in Christ. Being changed within and living a life of holiness as the Holy Spirit dwells in us and conforms us to the image of Christ.

**Soteriology** From the Greek words *soteria* (salvation) and *logos* (a word, a discourse). Thus a discourse on salvation (*see* Salvation). More broadly refers to the study of salvation. Salvation is the rescue from sin and its eternal result, which is being shut out of the immediate presence of the triune (*see* Triune) God (Rev 22:15) known as the Lake of Fire or hell. Yet, salvation is not to be seen as merely a blessed "end result." It entails much, such as reconciliation (*see* Reconciliation), holiness, justification (*see* Justification), etc., all things that occur in the present life and brought to full reality in the life to come.

**Theology** A discourse on God. Also refers to the study of God. From the words *theos* (*see* Theos) and *logos* (*see* Logos).

**Theos** The Greek word for "God."

**Transcendence (Transcendent)** In theology (*see* Theology), the doctrine (*see* Doctrine) that God is exalted above all things and ruler over all.

**Trinity** From "tri-unity" or "three in unity." The doctrine (*see* Doctrine) of "one being or God as three distinct persons; three distinct persons as one being or God." (*See* Being.)

**Trinitarian** When some thing or subject is characterized by the doctrine (*see* Doctrine) of the Trinity (*see* Trinity).

**Triune** Describes God as Trinity (*see* Trinity).

**Vicarious (Substitutionary)** Taking the place of another or others.

**Virgin Birth** *See* Virgin Conception and Birth.

**Virgin Conception and Birth** Refers to the incarnation (*see* Incarnation; *see* Conception) of Christ. Christ, having been sent by the Father, was conceived in the womb of the virgin Mary by the Holy Spirit.

**Western and Eastern Traditions** Two theological traditions. Generally the Western tradition comprises Protestant and Roman Catholic. The Eastern mainly consists of churches with the word "Orthodox" in their descriptions; thus Eastern Orthodox, Russian Orthodox, Greek Orthodox, etc.

**Western Theology** *See* Western and Eastern Traditions.

**Worship** Refers to a number of cognitive and physical actions expressed toward an object: Awe; adoration; respect; honor; thanksgiving; praise; prostration before; honoring, etc. We look to Jesus for our definition of worship. He worships the Father in communion with the Holy Spirit; and we participate *in* Jesus, *through* him, and *with* him in worshiping the Father in communion with the Holy Spirit. Further, we worship the Holy Trinity (*see* Trinity) in relationship with the Father and the Son and the Holy Spirit.

**Yahweh (Hebrew** YHWH) Translated "LORD" in modern translations (note the small caps). Whenever we see LORD, the Hebrew is *YHWH*.

# *Appendix*

## The Nicene-Constantinopolitan Creed[1]

We believe in one God the Father Almighty, maker of heaven and earth and of all that is seen and unseen.

We believe in one Lord Jesus Christ, the only Son of God, begotten of the Father from all eternity; Light from Light, true God from true God; begotten but not made; one Being[2] with the Father, through whom all things were made. For us and for our salvation he came down from heaven. By the power of the Holy Spirit he became incarnate from the Virgin Mary, and was made a man.

For our sake he was crucified under Pontius Pilate; he suffered death and was buried. On the third day he rose again according to the Scriptures; he ascended into heaven and is seated at the right hand of the Father. He will come again in glory to judge the living and the dead, and his kingdom will have no end.

We believe in the Holy Spirit, the Lord, the giver of life, who proceeds from the Father. With the Father and the Son he is worshiped and glorified. He has spoken through the Prophets.

---

1. See https://earlychurchtexts.com/public/nicene_creed.htm.
2. *Homo-ousios.*

We believe in one holy catholic and apostolic church. We confess one baptism for the forgiveness of sins. We wait in expectation for the resurrection of the dead, and the life of the world to come. Amen.

## The Creed of Chalcedon[3]

We, then, following the holy fathers, all with one consent, teach men to confess one and the same Son, our Lord Jesus Christ, the same perfect in Godhead and also perfect in manhood.

Truly God and truly man; of a reasonable [rational] soul and body; consubstantial[4] with the Father according to the Godhead, and consubstantial[5] with us according to the Manhood.

In all things like unto us, without sin.

Begotten before all ages of the Father according to the Godhead, and in these latter days, for us and for our salvation, born of the Virgin Mary, the Mother of God, according to the Manhood.

One and the same Christ, Son, Lord, Only-begotten, to be ac-knowledged in two natures, *inconfusedly, unchangeably, indivisi-bly, inseparably*; the distinction of natures being by no means taken away by the union, but rather the property of each nature being preserved, and concurring in one person and one subsistence, not parted or divided into two persons, but one and the same Son, and only begotten, God the Word, the Lord Jesus Christ, as the prophets from the beginning [have declared] concerning him, and the Lord Jesus Christ himself has taught us, and the Creed of the holy fathers has handed down to us.

---

3. See Philip Schaff, *The Creeds of Christendom.* https://www.ccel.org/ccel/schaff/creeds2.iv.i.iii.html.

4. *Homo-ousios.*

5. *Homo-ousios.*

# Bibliography

Athanasius. *Against the Arians*. A Select Library of Nicene and Post-Nicene Fathers of the Christian Church. Edited by Philip Schaff and Henry Wace. 28 vols. in 2 series. 1886–89. https://www.bible.ca/history/fathers/ NPNF2-04/Npnf2-04-60.htm#P6491_2577885.

———. *On Luke 10:22*. A Select Library of Nicene and Post-Nicene Fathers of the Christian Church. Edited by Philip Schaff and Henry Wace. 28 vols. in 2 series. 1886–89. https://www.bible.ca/history/fathers/NPNF2-04/ Npnf2-04-60.htm#P6491_2577885.

Aquinas, Thomas. *Summa Theologica*. https://d2y1pz2y630308.cloudfront. net/15471/documents/2016/10/St.%20Thomas%20Aquinas-Summa%20 Theologica.pdf.

Bavinck, Herman. *The Doctrine of God*. Carlisle, PA: Banner of Truth, 1977.

Erickson, Millard J. *Christian Theology*. Grand Rapids: Baker, 1985.

Hodge, A. A. *Outlines of Theology*. 1863. Reprint, Carlisle, PA: Banner of Truth, 1972.

Hodge, Charles. *Systematic Theology*. 3 vols. 1871–73. Reprint, Louisville: GLH, 2015.

Irenaeus. *Against Heresies*. https://www.bible.ca/history/fathers/ANF-01/ welcome.htm.

———. *Demonstration of the Apostolic Preaching*. https://www.documenta catholicaomnia.eu/03d/0130-0202,_Iraeneus,_Demonstration_Of_The_ Apostolic_Preaching,_EN.pdf.

Morton, Brooks St. Clair. *The Great CoMission: Making Sense of Making Disciples*. Lanham, MD: University Press of America, 2013.

Radcliff, Jason Robert. *Thomas F. Torrance and the Orthodox-Reformed Theological Dialogue*. Eugene, OR: Pickwick, 2018.

Rahner, Karl. *The Trinity*. London: Bloomsbury, 2001.

Richter, Sandra L. *The Epic of Eden: A Christian Entry into the Old Testament*. Downers Grove, IL: InterVarsity, 2008.

Sharp, Granville. *Remarks on the Uses of the Definite Article in the Greek Text of the New Testament*. https://archive.org/details/remarksonusesofdoosharrich/ page/n5/mode/2up.

Taylor, Justin. "Using a Diagram to Illustrate Trinitarian Relationships." https://www.thegospelcoalition.org/blogs/justin-taylor/using-a-diagram-to-illustrate-trinitarian-relationships.

Torrance, Thomas F. *The Christian Doctrine of God: One Being, Three Persons.* Edinburgh: T. & T. Clark, 1996.

————. *The Ground and Grammar of Theology.* Charlottesville: University of Virginia Press, 1980.

————. *Theology in Reconciliation: Essays towards Evangelical and Catholic Unity in East and West.* Eugene, OR: Wipf & Stock, 1996.

————. *The Trinitarian Faith: The Evangelical Theology of the Ancient Catholic Church.* Edinburgh: T. & T. Clark, 1995.

Tsoukalas, Steven. "Do Christians and Muslims Worship the Same God?" *Journal of the Evangelical Theological Society* 63.2 (2020) 303–30.

United Pentecostal Church International. "Our Beliefs." https://www.upci.org/about/our-beliefs.

Wiley, H. Orton, and Paul T. Culbertson. *Introduction to Christian Theology.* Kansas City, MO: Beacon Hill, 1946.

# Index

Made in the USA
Coppell, TX
24 August 2021